PRISM 1

LISTENING AND SPEAKING

Stephanie Dimond-Bayir
Kimberly Russell

with
Angela Blackwell
Carolyn Flores

CAMBRIDGE
UNIVERSITY PRESS

CAMBRIDGE
UNIVERSITY PRESS

University Printing House, Cambridge CB2 8BS, United Kingdom

One Liberty Plaza, 20th Floor, New York, NY 10006, USA

477 Williamstown Road, Port Melbourne, VIC 3207, Australia

4843/24, 2nd Floor, Ansari Road, Daryaganj, Delhi – 110002, India

79 Anson Road, #06–04/06, Singapore 079906

Cambridge University Press is part of the University of Cambridge.

It furthers the University's mission by disseminating knowledge in the pursuit of education, learning and research at the highest international levels of excellence.

www.cambridge.org
Information on this title: www.cambridge.org/9781316620946

First published 2017

20 19 18 17 16 15 14 13 12 11 10 9 8 7 6 5 4 3 2 1

Printed in Dubai by Oriental Press

A catalogue record for this publication is available from the British Library

ISBN 978-1-316-62094-6 Student's Book with Online Workbook 1 Listening and Speaking
ISBN 978-1-316-62511-8 Teacher's Manual 1 Listening and Speaking

Cambridge University Press has no responsibility for the persistence or accuracy of URLs for external or third-party internet websites referred to in this publication, and does not guarantee that any content on such websites is, or will remain, accurate or appropriate. Information regarding prices, travel timetables, and other factual information given in this work is correct at the time of first printing but Cambridge University Press does not guarantee the accuracy of such information thereafter.

CONTENTS

SCOPE AND SEQUENCE

UNIT	WATCH AND LISTEN	LISTENINGS	LISTENING SKILLS	PRONUNCIATION FOR LISTENING	
1 PLACES *Academic Disciplines* Sociology / Urban Planning	The Grand Canal	1: A podcast about homes around the world 2: A profile on Stanley Park in Vancouver	*Key Skills* Predicting content using visuals Distinguishing fact from opinion *Additional Skills* Understanding key vocabulary Predicting content using visuals Listening for main ideas Listening for details Taking notes Synthesizing	Vowel sounds /eɪ/, /ɒ/, /ɪ/, /ʌ/	
2 FESTIVALS AND CELEBRATIONS *Academic Disciplines* Anthropology / Cultural Studies / Sociology	Harbin's Ice Festival	1: Interviews about three cultural festivals 2: A discussion about Thanksgiving in the U.S. and Canada	*Key Skills* Taking notes Listening for main ideas *Additional Skills* Understanding key vocabulary Predicting content using visuals Listening for details Recognizing examples Synthesizing	Word stress	
3 THE INTERNET AND TECHNOLOGY *Academic Disciplines* Computer science / Engineering	Fiber Optic Cables	1: A student radio program about developments in robotics 2: A news report about how computers affect memory	*Key Skill* Listening for reasons *Additional Skills* Understanding key vocabulary Using your knowledge Predicting content using visuals Listening for main ideas Listening for details Taking notes Synthesizing	Consonant sounds /s/, /ʃ/, /ʧ/ Strong /æ/ and weak /ə/	
4 WEATHER AND CLIMATE *Academic Disciplines* Ecology / Environmental Studies / Psychology	The Impact of Oceans on Climate	1: A student discussion on how weather affects people's moods 2: A news report on global warming and its effects on rainforests	*Key Skill* Predicting ideas from research *Additional Skills* Understanding key vocabulary Using your knowledge Predicting content using visuals Listening for main ideas Listening for details Taking notes Synthesizing	Rising and falling intonation Vowel sounds /ɑ/ and /oʊ/	

LANGUAGE DEVELOPMENT	CRITICAL THINKING	SPEAKING	ON CAMPUS
Review of the simple past Descriptive adjectives	Planning a presentation Evaluating opinions	***Speaking Skills*** Signposting an opinion Organizing information for a presentation ***Pronunciation*** Connecting speech ***Speaking Task*** Give a presentation about an interesting place.	***Life Skill*** Campus resources
Gerunds and infinitives Collocations with *go to*, *take*, and *have*	Organizing ideas Analyzing and evaluating options	***Speaking Skills*** Making suggestions Agreeing and disagreeing ***Speaking Task*** Choose a group of events from a festival and persuade your group to go to them.	***Communication Skill*** Starting and continuing a conversation
Can / be able to Vocabulary for technology	Evaluating and categorizing advantages and disadvantages	***Speaking Skill*** Giving additional and contrasting information ***Speaking Task*** Present a report about a device or technology.	***Study Skill*** Technology for learning
Verb collocations Future forms	Evaluating effects	***Speaking Skill*** Linking words to explain cause and effect ***Speaking Task*** Give a presentation about changes in the climate.	***Life Skill*** Managing your time

UNIT	WATCH AND LISTEN	LISTENINGS	LISTENING SKILLS	PRONUNCIATION FOR LISTENING
5 SPORTS AND COMPETITION _Academic Disciplines_ Sports Management / Sports Science	Kasparov versus Deep Blue	1: A student presentation on unusual sports 2: A discussion about money in sports	_Key Skill_ Listening for bias Supporting opinions _Additional Skills_ Understanding key vocabulary Listening for main ideas Listening for details Listening for opinion Taking notes Synthesizing	Making corrections
6 BUSINESS _Academic Disciplines_ Business / Marketing	Food at Coffee Shops	1: A conversation between a business student and a professor about a project 2: A conversation between a business owner and a consultant	_Key Skill_ Listening for numbers _Additional Skills_ Understanding key vocabulary Using your knowledge Listening for details Listening for reaction Making inferences Taking notes Synthesizing	Pronouncing numbers
7 PEOPLE _Academic Disciplines_ Psychology / Sociology	Trash Artists	1: A student presentation on creative people 2: A student conversation about a project	_Key Skill_ Listening for attitude _Additional Skills_ Understanding key vocabulary Using your knowledge Listening for main ideas Listening for details Taking notes Synthesizing	Intonation for emotion and interest
8 THE UNIVERSE _Academic Disciplines_ Astronomy / Engineering	Empire of the Sun	1: A radio program about space travel 2: A discussion on funding for space exploration	_Key Skill_ Understanding meaning from context _Additional Skills_ Understanding key vocabulary Predicting content using visuals Listening for details Listening to an introduction Taking notes Synthesizing	Words with easily confused sounds

LANGUAGE DEVELOPMENT	CRITICAL THINKING	SPEAKING	ON CAMPUS
Factual and future real conditionals Adverbs of degree	Analyzing reasons and supporting evidence Using a persuasion map	***Speaking Skills*** Presenting a point Asking for and giving clarification ***Speaking Task*** Have a discussion about money in sports. Discuss reasons for and against athletes being paid extremely large amounts of money.	***Communication Skill*** Asking for information
Comparatives and superlatives Phrasal verbs	Using problem and solution charts Analyzing and evaluating problems and possible solutions	***Speaking Skill*** Giving advice ***Speaking Task*** Give advice to a failing business.	***Communication Skill*** Working in groups

Adjective endings
  -ed and *-ing*
The past progressive:
  • Forming the past progressive
  • The past progressive and the simple past
	Using an idea map
	Analyzing qualities
		Speaking Skills
		Time order
		Examples and details
		Speaking Task
		Give a presentation about a remarkable person and his or her work.
			Presentation Skill
			Giving presentations

Vocabulary for problems and solutions Future unreal conditionals	Analyzing a problem Evaluating possible solutions to a problem Using a problem and solution chart	***Speaking Skills*** Turn-taking Showing levels of agreement ***Speaking Task*** Discuss how to get children interested in space exploration.	***Study Skill*** Reviewing for exams

HOW *PRISM* WORKS

1 Video

Setting the context

Every unit begins with a video clip. Each video serves as a springboard for the unit and introduces the topic in an engaging way. The clips were carefully selected to pique students' interest and prepare them to explore the unit's topic in greater depth. As they work, students develop key skills in prediction, comprehension, and discussion.

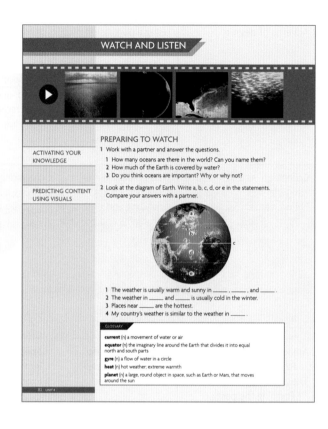

2 Listening

Receptive, language, and analytical skills

Students improve their listening abilities through a sequence of proven activities. They study key vocabulary to prepare them for each listening and to develop academic listening skills. Pronunciation for Listening exercises help students learn how to decode spoken English. Language Development sections teach grammar and vocabulary. A second listening leads into synthesis exercises that prepare students for college classrooms.

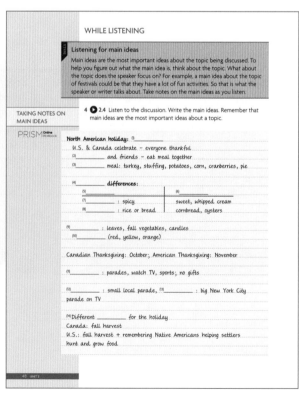

PREPARATION FOR SPEAKING

PRESENTING POINTS AND CLARIFYING STATEMENTS

Presenting a point

When you discuss a topic with others, you can use signal words to help you make that point strongly.

Of course, obviously, actually, and *definitely* all signal to the listener that what comes next is going to be a point that you wish to emphasize.

PRISM Online Workbook

1 ▶ 5.5 Listen to the sentences from Listening 2. Use the words from the box to complete the sentences.

actually	definitely	obviously	of course

1 I think there is _____ more marketing and business in sports than ever before.

2 And _____ , only about 5 percent of Olympic athletes get money from big companies to be in ads.

3 Well, _____ poorer countries can't usually pay the costs for training athletes.

4 And _____ , the countries with lots of money can train their athletes really well.

2 Write sentences to give reasons and support either for or against the points you made in Exercises 4 and 5 in Critical Thinking. Use a word from the box above to emphasize your point in each sentence.

Sports fans actually like to see ads with athletes in them.

a _____

b _____

c _____

d _____

3 Work with a partner who chose the same point of view as you in Exercise 2. Share your sentences. Discuss your argument, reasons, and support. Do you have similar ideas?

38 UNIT 5

3 Speaking

Critical thinking and production

Multiple critical thinking activities begin this section, setting students up for exercises that focus on speaking skills, functional language, and pronunciation. All of these lead up to a structured speaking task, in which students apply the skills and language they have developed over the course of the entire unit.

ON CAMPUS

CAMPUS RESOURCES

PREPARING TO LISTEN

1 Look at the map and find the places below. Which of the places do you have on your campus?

the library   residence halls   parking   the gym   the theater
the Student Union   the Administration building

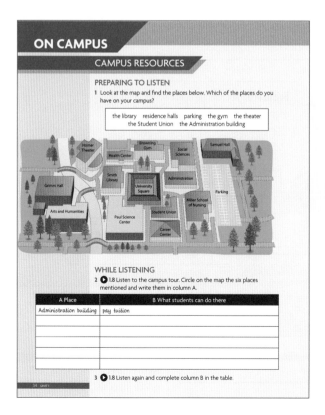

WHILE LISTENING

2 ▶ 1.8 Listen to the campus tour. Circle on the map the six places mentioned and write them in column A.

A Place	B What students can do there
Administration building	pay tuition

3 ▶ 1.8 Listen again and complete column B in the table.

34 UNIT 1

4 On Campus

Skills for college life

This unique section teaches students valuable skills beyond academic listening and speaking. From asking questions in class to participating in a study group and from being an active listener to finding help, students learn how to navigate university life. The section begins with a context-setting listening, and moves directly into active practice of the skill.

WHAT MAKES *PRISM* SPECIAL: CRITICAL THINKING

Bloom's Taxonomy

In order to truly prepare for college coursework, students need to develop a full range of thinking skills. *Prism* teaches explicit critical thinking skills in every unit of every level. These skills adhere to the taxonomy developed by Benjamin Bloom. By working within the taxonomy, we are able to ensure that your students learn both lower-order and higher-order thinking skills.

Critical thinking exercises are accompanied by icons indicating where the activities fall in Bloom's Taxonomy.

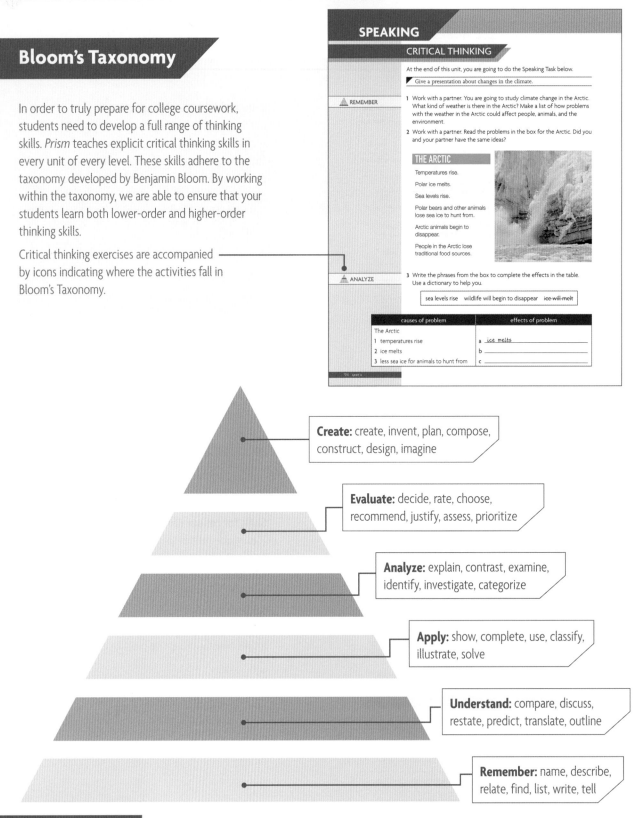

SPEAKING

CRITICAL THINKING

At the end of this unit, you are going to do the Speaking Task below.

Give a presentation about changes in the climate.

REMEMBER

1 Work with a partner. You are going to study climate change in the Arctic. What kind of weather is there in the Arctic? Make a list of how problems with the weather in the Arctic could affect people, animals, and the environment.

2 Work with a partner. Read the problems in the box for the Arctic. Did you and your partner have the same ideas?

THE ARCTIC

Temperatures rise.

Polar ice melts.

Sea levels rise.

Polar bears and other animals lose sea ice to hunt from.

Arctic animals begin to disappear.

People in the Arctic lose traditional food sources.

ANALYZE

3 Write the phrases from the box to complete the effects in the table. Use a dictionary to help you.

sea levels rise   wildlife will begin to disappear   ice will melt

causes of problem	effects of problem
The Arctic	
1 temperatures rise	a _ice melts_
2 ice melts	b _____
3 less sea ice for animals to hunt from	c _____

Create: create, invent, plan, compose, construct, design, imagine

Evaluate: decide, rate, choose, recommend, justify, assess, prioritize

Analyze: explain, contrast, examine, identify, investigate, categorize

Apply: show, complete, use, classify, illustrate, solve

Understand: compare, discuss, restate, predict, translate, outline

Remember: name, describe, relate, find, list, write, tell

WHAT MAKES *PRISM* SPECIAL: CRITICAL THINKING

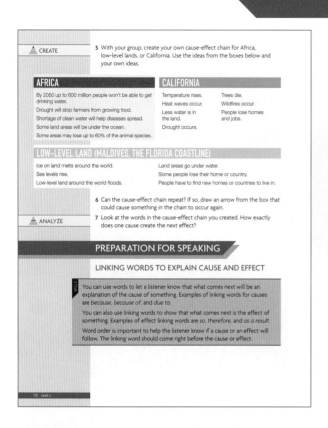

Higher-Order Thinking Skills

Create, **Evaluate**, and **Analyze** are critical skills for students in any college setting. Academic success depends on their abilities to derive knowledge from collected data, make educated judgments, and deliver insightful presentations. *Prism* helps students get there by creating activities such as categorizing information, comparing data, selecting the best solution to a problem, and developing arguments for a discussion or presentation.

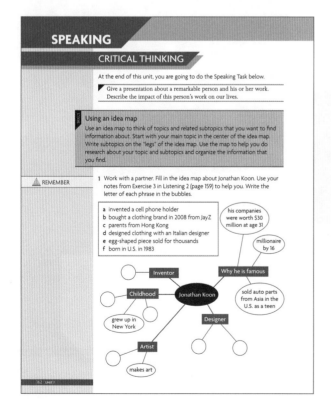

Lower-Order Thinking Skills

Apply, **Understand**, and **Remember** provide the foundation upon which all thinking occurs. Students need to be able to recall information, comprehend it, and see its use in new contexts. *Prism* develops these skills through exercises such as taking notes, mining notes for specific data, demonstrating comprehension, and distilling information from charts.

WHAT MAKES *PRISM* SPECIAL: ON CAMPUS

More college skills
Students need more than traditional academic skills. *Prism* teaches important skills for being engaged and successful all around campus, from emailing professors to navigating study groups.

Professors
Students learn how to take good lecture notes and how to communicate with professors and academic advisors.

Beyond the classroom
Skills include how to utilize campus resources, where to go for help, how to choose classes, and more.

Active learning
Students practice participating in class, in online discussion boards, and in study groups.

Texts
Learners become proficient at taking notes and annotating textbooks as well as conducting research online and in the library.

COLLOCATIONS

A collocation is a combination of two or more words that are often used together.
go to college, go to a talk, go to class

PRISM Online Workbook

4 Label each circle with the correct words from the box to make verb + noun collocations. Some words can be used more than once.

a celebration (x2)	care	college	a concert	an event (x2)	
a festival	fun	a good time	a lecture	a party (x2)	
part	place	a photo	a problem	a video	your time

5 Write the correct form of *go to, have,* or *take.*

1 Excuse me, can you _____ a photo of my sister and me?
2 What time will you leave your house to _____ the celebration?
3 I'm going on vacation next week. Will you _____ care of my plants?
4 _____ a good time on your vacation!
5 I'm sorry that I can't go to your party tonight. But I hope you _____ fun!

6 Write the correct form of the words from Exercise 4. In some items, more than one answer is possible.

1 What do you think makes a good festival? Should everyone go to every _____, or is it OK to miss some of them?
2 Do you take _____ to enjoy a festival when you go, or do you hurry to see things?
3 In your country do people often go to _____ to listen to music?
4 If it's your birthday, do you have a _____ ?

7 Work with a partner. Ask and answer the questions.

46 UNIT 2

Vocabulary Research

Learning the right words

Students need to learn a wide range of general and academic vocabulary in order to be successful in college. *Prism* carefully selects the vocabulary that students study based on the General Service List, the Academic Word List, and the Cambridge English Corpus.

LISTENING

LISTENING 1

PRONUNCIATION FOR LISTENING

Rising and falling intonation
Intonation describes how the tone of your voice goes up (rises) and goes down (falls). Intonation can help you understand someone's mood (e.g., happy, interested, excited, bored, sad, upset, etc.). Rising intonation can show interest or happiness. Falling intonation often shows boredom or sadness. Falling intonation can also show certainty.

really = The speaker is interested.

really = The speaker is not interested.

The meaning of a sentence can change depending on the intonation. Read the sentence aloud with a rising intonation and then a falling intonation. How does the meaning change?
I know.

PRISM Online Workbook

1 ▶ 4.1 Listen to the dialogues. Write *I* (interested) or *B* (bored) for Speaker B.

1 A: Did you know global warming is still increasing?
   B: Is it? _____
2 A: It's my birthday today.
   B: Really? Happy birthday! _____
3 A: The weather got really chilly, didn't it?
   B: I suppose so. _____
4 A: Thanks for inviting me to your party!
   B: You're welcome. It'll be nice to see you! _____
5 A: Dinner was great.
   B: Good. Glad you liked it. _____

2 Work with a partner. Read the dialogues aloud. Speaker B should change their intonation. Speaker A should guess whether Speaker B sounds interested or bored.

84 UNIT 4

Pronunciation for Listening

Training your ears

This unique feature teaches learners to listen for specific features of spoken English that typically inhibit comprehension. Learners become primed to better understand detail and nuance while listening.

LEARNING OBJECTIVES

Listening skills	Predict content using visuals; distinguish fact from opinion
Pronunciation	Vowel sounds /eɪ/, /ɒ/, /ɪ/, /ʌ/; connect speech
Speaking skills	Signpost an opinion; organize information for a presentation
Speaking Task	Give a presentation about an interesting place
On Campus	Campus resources

ACTIVATE YOUR KNOWLEDGE

Work with a partner. Look at the photo and answer the questions.

1 Would you prefer to live in a house or an apartment building? Why?

2 Do you think the apartments in the photo are unusual? Why?

3 Why do people choose to live in unusual places?

4 What are some of the advantages of living near the ocean? On a mountain? In a downtown area?

PREPARING TO WATCH

ACTIVATING YOUR KNOWLEDGE

1 Work with a partner and answer the questions.

1 Where is the city of Venice?
2 What do you know about Venice?
3 Why do tourists like to visit old towns or cities like Venice?

PREDICTING CONTENT USING VISUALS

2 You are going to watch a video about Venice. Look at the pictures from the video. Work with a partner. Discuss how this city looks different from other cities.

> **GLOSSARY**
>
> **canal** (n) a river made by people
>
> **gondola** (n) a narrow boat with a raised point at both ends, used on canals in Venice
>
> **man-made** (adj) not natural, but made by people
>
> **palace** (n) a large, important house or building, often where a king or queen lives
>
> **stilts** (n) long pieces of wood or metal that a building stands on so that it is above the ground or water

WHILE WATCHING

UNDERSTANDING MAIN IDEAS

3 ▶ Watch the video. Write *T* (true) or *F* (false) next to the statements. Correct the false statements.

_____ 1 Venice does not have many beautiful churches.
_____ 2 There are a lot of canals and bridges.
_____ 3 Most of the islands between the canals are big.
_____ 4 Today, Venice is important for art and businesses.
_____ 5 People know Venice as a popular tourist center.
_____ 6 The Grand Canal is the smallest canal in Venice.
_____ 7 The Grand Canal is a man-made river.
_____ 8 Another name for Venice is "The City of Boats."

4 ▶ Read the questions. Then watch the video again and answer the questions.

1 What does Venice have instead of busy roads?
2 What don't you see on them?
3 What is the name of the special boats in the video?
4 What are palaces and other buildings in Venice built on?
5 What was the Ca' d'Oro palace decorated with?
6 What is the Rialto Bridge made of?

5 Work with a partner. Complete each sentence with a number from the box.

one   two   15   117   300   400

1 There are _____ islands between the canals, and _____ bridges in Venice.
2 The Grand Canal is more than _____ miles long.
3 For nearly _____ years, you could only cross the Grand Canal on the Rialto Bridge.
4 The Ca' d'Oro is _____ of Venice's most beautiful palaces.
5 The palace was built in the _____th century.

6 Work with a partner. The speaker in the video says that a gondola ride is "one of the best 30 minutes you can spend in your life."

1 Why do you think the speaker says this?
2 Do you agree with his opinion? Why or why not?

DISCUSSION

7 Work in a small group. Discuss the questions.

1 What do you think it is like to live in Venice?
2 Does your hometown or country have any interesting canals, rivers, or roads?

8 Look at the advertisement about gondola boat rides. Answer the questions.

1 Can you take a boat ride on Monday night?
2 Is there a boat ride at 10:00 in the morning?
3 Where does the boat ride begin?
4 How much does it cost?
5 Why do you think the boat rides are from April until October?
6 Why do the boats have life jackets?

Gondola Boat Rides

Starting at the Ca' d'Oro Palace
Every day of the week
11:00 a.m., 2:00 p.m., 3:00 p.m.

€20 per person

from April to October

We have life jackets for everyone!

LISTENING

LISTENING 1

PREPARING TO LISTEN

1 Read the sentences. Write the words in bold next to the definitions.

1 Look at the pictures. Do you **recognize** any of the places? Where are they?
2 Some of these places are very **strange**. They are not like other places.
3 The **capital** of the United States is Washington, D.C. The president lives there.
4 These **ancient** buildings are more than 1,000 years old.
5 Mountains have a lot of **rocks** on them. It is difficult to walk around them. They make it difficult to walk.
6 Kara lives in a small **apartment** in New York City. It's in a big building.
7 We have to drive over the **bridge** to get to the island.
8 Lisa found a large **cave** on the mountain. It was very dark and cold inside.

a _____ (adj) different from the usual or normal; unusual or not expected
b _____ (n) something built over a river or road that lets people, cars, or trains go across
c _____ (n) a hard piece of the material that the Earth is made of
d _____ (v) to know something because you have seen it before
e _____ (n) a large hole in the side of a mountain or under the ground
f _____ (adj) from a long time ago; very old
g _____ (n) a room or set of rooms in a building for someone to live in
h _____ (n) the most important city in a country or state, where the government is

---

SKILLS

Predicting content using visuals

Before you listen, look quickly at the pictures related to the listening. Think of important or "key" words to describe the pictures. This helps you understand more about the topic when you listen.

2 You are going to listen to a podcast about homes around the world. Look at the photos. What do you think you will learn about homes?

3 Work with a partner. Look at the photos. Match the words from the box to the photos. In some items, more than one answer is possible.

| an-cient | bri̱dge | ca̱ve | ro̱ck | stra̱nge |

PRONUNCIATION FOR LISTENING

Vowel sounds /eɪ/, /ɒ/, /ɪ/, /ʌ/

Pronunciation is just as important for listening as it is for speaking. When you improve your English pronunciation, you also improve your ability to understand others when you are listening.

▶ 1.1 Listen to each of the words below. Notice the different vowel sounds in each word.

/eɪ/ pl<u>a</u>ce   /ɒ/ h<u>o</u>t   /ɪ/ qu<u>i</u>ck   /ʌ/ <u>u</u>p

PRISM Online Workbook

4 Work with a partner. Say the words from the table and notice the underlined sound. Write the words from Exercise 3 in the table.

/eɪ/	/ɒ/	/ɪ/	/ʌ/
pl<u>a</u>ce	h<u>o</u>t	qu<u>i</u>ck	<u>u</u>p

5 Write the words from the box in the table in Exercise 4.

bu<u>i</u>lt   h<u>u</u>n-dreds   l<u>o</u>ng   <u>u</u>n-der   s<u>ay</u>

6 Work with a partner. Take turns reading aloud different words from the lists below. Your partner should listen carefully and tell you which word you said.

Student A: Cut.
Student B: You said cut. Number 2. List D.

	A	B	C	D
1	hate	hot	hit	hut
2	Kate	cot	kit	cut

WHILE LISTENING

7 ▶ 1.2 Look at the questions. Listen and circle the correct answer.

LISTENING FOR
MAIN IDEAS

1 The speakers on the podcast are
   a scientists.
   b professors.
   c world travelers.
2 The main topic of the podcast is
   a traveling to different countries.
   b unusual places where people live.
   c a history of ancient houses.

8 ▶ 1.2 Listen to the podcast again and complete the student's notes. Then compare your notes with a partner.

TAKING NOTES
ON DETAILS

- Matmata is in (1)_____ .
  Matmata facts: (2)_____ years old. (3)_____ miles south of Tunis.
- Cappadocia is in (4)_____ .
  Cappadocia facts: caves formed about (5)_____ years ago.
- Ponte Vecchio is in (6)_____ .
  Ponte Vecchio facts: built in (7)_____ .
- Neft Dashlari is in (8)_____ .
  Neft Dashlari facts: bridge is (9)_____ miles long.
  (10)_____ people live there.

DISCUSSION

9 Choose one of the topics and discuss it with a partner.

1 Describe the most interesting building you know. Do you think it would be a good place for people to visit on vacation? Why or why not?
2 Would you like to live in any of the places described in the podcast? Why or why not?

REVIEW OF THE SIMPLE PAST

LANGUAGE

Simple past statements

Use *the simple past* to talk about events that happened in the past. For regular verbs, add -ed to the base form. Add -d to verbs that end in -e. Use the same form for all persons (*I, you, we, they, he, she, it*).

They **filmed** some scenes from a movie there. (film → film**ed**)
She **lived** there for 20 years. (live → live**d**)

Memorize past forms of irregular verbs.

They **made** them out of rock. (make → **made**)
I **saw** some tall apartment buildings. (see → **saw**)
I **went** to Turkey. (go → **went**)
They **built** the bridge in 1345. (build → **built**)
They **put** houses there. (put → **put**)

For negative statements in the simple past, use *did + not* or *didn't* and the base form of the verb. (*did not = didn't*)

They **did not live** in Dubai for a long time.
I **didn't see** much of Seoul.

Be is an irregular verb. The past forms of *be* are *was / were*. Use *was* with *I / he / she / it*. Use *were* with *you / we / they*.

When I **was** younger, I went to Turkey.
They **were** very strange buildings.

For negative statements with *be*, use *wasn't* or *weren't*.

They **weren't** there for a long time.
Marco **wasn't** in Mexico City last week.

PRISM Online Workbook

1 Circle the verbs in the simple past in the sentences from Listening 1. In some sentences, there is more than one answer.

  1 People changed them into homes during the Roman period.
  2 ... I went to Cappadocia in Turkey.
  3 So they made this one ...
  4 There was another bridge there before, but an accident destroyed it.
  5 They decided that the workers needed somewhere to live, so they built a kind of "city" above the sea.
  6 They put houses, libraries, schools, and even a movie theater there.
  7 The caves formed from rock more than 8,000 years ago.

2 Complete the table with the simple past of the verbs from Exercise 1.

simple past verbs: regular (add -*ed*)	simple past verbs: irregular
changed	went

3 Answer the questions. Use the simple past.

1 Where did you live when you were a child?

_____

2 When did you start to live in your home?

_____

3 Where was your mother's home when she was a child?

_____

4 Where did you go on your last vacation?

_____

5 Did you know the people who lived near you when you were a child?

_____

6 How often did you change the color of your bedroom walls when you were young?

_____

4 Work with a partner. Choose two of the questions from Exercise 3 to ask your partner. Take turns asking and answering questions.

DESCRIPTIVE ADJECTIVES

5 Label the pictures with the words from the box. Use a dictionary to help you.

> ancient   cheap   crowded   expensive
> modern   popular   rural   urban

a _____   b _____   c _____   d _____

e _____   f _____   g _____   h _____

6 Think about Neft Dashlari. There are houses, libraries, schools, and even a movie theater, all built on a long bridge. Do you think this was an *expensive* or a *cheap* place to build?

7 Write the correct words in the sentences.

1 The city of Los Angeles is a large _____ (*rural / urban*) area.
2 Many people like to visit Niagara Falls, so we can say that it is a(n) _____ (*urban / popular*) place to go.
3 The state of Montana has very few cities and a lot of farms. It is one of the most _____ (*rural / urban*) places in the U.S.
4 New York City is a really _____ (*cheap / expensive*) place to live. The cost to live there is very high.

8 Work with a partner. Take turns choosing words from Exercise 5. Give an example of a place or thing that can be described by each word you choose to help your partner guess the word.

Student A: The Great Wall of China is like this.
Student B: Is it ancient?

PREPARING TO LISTEN

UNDERSTANDING
KEY VOCABULARY

PRISM Online Workbook

1 Read the sentences. Write the words in bold next to the definitions.

1 I like to live in **urban** places. There are lots of very tall buildings and a lot of fun things to do.

2 In the summer you can swim in a **lake** if you get hot.

3 When I go to the **woods**, I can see many birds and other wild animals.

4 Tokyo is a **modern** city with public transportation and a lot of new buildings.

5 What **area** of the city do you live in, uptown or downtown?

6 Los Angeles has a lot of **traffic** because so many people there drive cars every day.

7 A **field** in a park is a nice place to sit and relax because it is open and sunny.

8 The city of Vancouver is **located** in British Columbia in western Canada.

a _____ (n) open, grassy land

b _____ (n) a part of a larger place

c _____ (adj) relating to the present time and not to the past

d _____ (n) a body of water that has land all around it

e _____ (n) all the cars and trucks using the road

f _____ (adj) belonging to or related to a city

g _____ (n) a place with a lot of trees growing near each other

h _____ (adj) in a certain place

PREDICTING CONTENT
USING VISUALS

2 Work with a partner. Look at the photo. Choose words from Exercise 1 to describe the photo. What do you think the lecture will be about?

WHILE LISTENING

3 ▶ 1.3 Listen to the lecture. Check your answers to Exercise 2. What was the lecture about?

a reasons to visit Vancouver, British Columbia
b the advantages and disadvantages of lots of parks in a city
c different things you can do in Stanley Park

4 ▶ 1.3 Listen to the lecture again. According to the speaker, what are the advantages of Stanley Park? What are the disadvantages? Take notes in the chart.

advantages	disadvantages
lots of gardens, walking paths, trees, and animals	

SKILLS

Distinguishing fact from opinion

It is important to understand if a speaker is giving a fact (a general truth about something) or an opinion (his or her personal feelings about something). Listen for signal words and phrases that can help you decide if you hear a fact or an opinion. Sometimes you will not hear signal words, so it is important to also listen for context.

5 ▶ 1.4 Listen and complete the sentences with the signal words and phrases you hear. Are the sentences facts or the speaker's opinions? Write _F_ (fact) or _O_ (opinion).

1 _Obviously_ , Stanley Park is a large park. __F__
2 _____ , because it is located in the city of Vancouver, it is the third largest urban park in North America. _____
3 _____ , lots of trees help clean the city air. _____
4 Finally, while _____ these disadvantages might mean that some people would not want to visit Vancouver, ... _____
5 ... _____ that most people would enjoy Vancouver. _____
6 _____ , being close to nature and having a healthy city are worth paying a little more money. _____

POST-LISTENING

6 Look at the signal words and phrases for fact and opinion in Exercise 5. Which tense is often used to give facts?

7 The signal words and phrases from Exercise 5 tell you if the information is a general fact or the opinion of the speaker. Add the phrases to the grouping diagrams.

FACT

Obviously ...

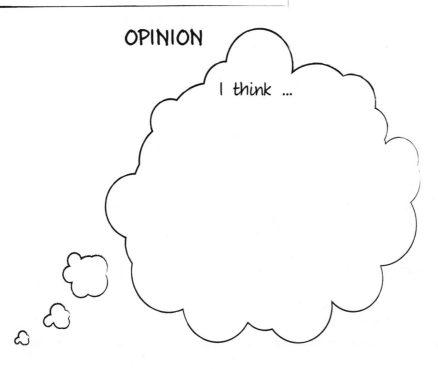

OPINION

I think ...

8 Speakers do not always use signal words to show facts and opinions. Read the sentences from the lecture. Write *F* (fact) or *O* (opinion). Check your answers with a partner.

1 Vancouver has the best parts of green forests and city life. _____
2 It has many gardens, walking paths, trees, and even animals like bald eagles, coyotes, and seals. _____
3 At the first city meeting, the people of Vancouver asked the national government to give the city 1,000 acres to use as a park.
4 It is one of the most beautiful cities in the world. _____

DISCUSSION

9 Work with a partner. What are some advantages of living in a big city? What are some disadvantages?

SYNTHESIZING

10 Work with a partner. Use your notes from Listening 1 and Listening 2 to answer the questions: Which of the places in Listening 1 and Listening 2 would you live in? Which ones would you only visit? Why?

SPEAKING

CRITICAL THINKING

At the end of this unit, you are going to do the Speaking Task below.

> Give a presentation about an interesting place. Present factual information and give your opinion about the place you choose.

Planning a presentation

Use a table to plan your presentation so that it is well organized and you have enough to say. Add sections for an introduction, general facts about your topic, your opinions (for example, positives and negatives), and a summary.

1 Work with a partner. Imagine you are going to describe Stanley Park in Vancouver to your class. Complete the presentation outline about Stanley Park. Use your notes from Listening 2 and the photo of Stanley Park on page 25 to help you.

ANALYZE ▲

plan for presentation	information
1 **introduction and general facts** Name of place / country / location	
2 **facts** How old / Who made it? Other events?	
3 **opinion (positives)** Interesting / Beautiful? Why visit?	
4 **opinion (negatives)** Expensive / Too crowded? Problems?	
5 **summary** Good? Go or not?	

2 Compare your presentation outlines with another pair. Use your notes in the table and explain your opinions about why you would or would not visit Stanley Park. Give reasons. Ask follow-up questions.

EVALUATE ▲

3 Choose an interesting place you know. Try to think of a place that other people might not know very well.

4 Find out some facts about the place you chose. Take notes on your own ideas and opinions about the place. Look for an interesting photo of the place.

5 Write an outline for a presentation about the place. Use the table to help you organize your presentation.

plan for presentation	information
1 introduction and general facts Name of place / country / location	
2 facts How old / Who made it? Other events?	
3 opinion (positives) Interesting / Beautiful? Why visit?	
4 opinion (negatives) Expensive / Too crowded? Problems?	
5 summary Good? Go or not?	

PREPARATION FOR SPEAKING

SIGNPOSTING AN OPINION

When you give your opinion, it is useful to start your sentence with a word or phrase that lets listeners know right away that you are giving your opinion and not stating a fact. It gets them ready to listen for what is coming next. It helps them think about your opinion and if they agree or not.

I personally feel that most people would enjoy Vancouver.
It seems to me that a lot of people agree with this idea ...

1 Work with a partner. Read the topic suggestions in the box. Take turns giving your opinion about two of the topics using signal words and phrases. Ask questions for more information.

> parks in a town or city   traffic in a town or city
> things to do in a town or city

Student A: In my opinion, this town has really bad traffic.
Student B: Why is there bad traffic?
Student A: I think it's because a lot of people live here, but there are only a few main roads. They're really small, too.

ORGANIZING INFORMATION FOR A PRESENTATION

2 When you present information, it is important to organize what you say into different topics so the listener can easily follow your ideas. Match the topics to the sentences.

1 general fact
2 positives
3 negatives
4 summary

a Parks give people places to walk, so they are healthier.
b Having many parks means there is less space to build houses.
c Life in Vancouver has more positives than negatives.
d Europeans came to live in Vancouver in the 1800s.

PRISM Online Workbook

3 ▶ 1.5 Here is some language that you can use to help your listener understand your ideas. Listen and circle the organizing phrase you hear.

1 *I'd like to talk about / I'd like to tell you about* the city of Vancouver, in British Columbia, Canada.
2 *First of all / Firstly*, let's look at some of the advantages.
3 *I'd also like to talk about / I'd also like to give you* some disadvantages of Stanley Park and Vancouver.
4 *In summary / Finally*, while I think these disadvantages mean that some people would not want to visit Vancouver, I personally feel that most people would enjoy Vancouver.

PRONUNCIATION FOR SPEAKING

SKILLS

Connecting speech

When you speak, words often link together to make your speech flow smoothly. To do this, the sounds at the end of one word and at the beginning of another may change.

One way this happens is when you connect (link) vowels and consonants. When one word ends in a consonant sound and the next word begins with a vowel sound, there is a link between them. For example, *talk about* becomes /tɑːkəbaʊt/.

▶ 1.6 Listen to this example. Notice that the words *talk* and *about* are connected.

I'd like to talk about the city of Vancouver, in British Columbia, Canada.

4 ▶ 1.7 Listen to the sentence below. Draw the links between the consonants and vowels.

> First of all, let's look at some of the advantages.

5 ▶ 1.5 Listen and repeat the phrases in Exercise 3. Pay attention to the way you link the words together.

6 Work with a partner. Mark the links in the phrases. Then take turns saying the phrases.

1 I'd like to give some information about ...
2 Now let's talk about ...
3 The next topic is ...
4 Finally, let's look at ...

SPEAKING TASK

> Give a presentation about an interesting place. Present factual information and give your opinion about the place you choose.

PREPARE

1 Look at the outline you created in Exercise 5 in Critical Thinking. Review your notes and add any new information.

2 Write a script for your introduction and conclusion. Be sure to use organizing phrases from Preparation for Speaking so your audience can easily understand your presentation.

3 For each idea in your presentation, think of how you can signal facts and your opinions. You can use language like this:

Obviously, ...   In my opinion, ...
In fact, ...   It seems ...

4 Refer to the Task Checklist below as you prepare your presentation.

TASK CHECKLIST	✔
Use the simple past correctly.	
Organize your presentation using appropriate organizing phrases.	
Introduce facts and opinions using the correct language.	
Join sounds in phrases when the words link together.	

PRESENT

5 Work in a group of three or four. Present your information to each other. While listening, take notes on questions that you have so you can ask them after the presentation is over.

6 Vote for the place that most students would like to visit.

CAMPUS RESOURCES

PREPARING TO LISTEN

1 Look at the map and find the places below. Which of the places do you have on your campus?

> the library   residence halls   parking   the gym   the theater
> the Student Union   the Administration building

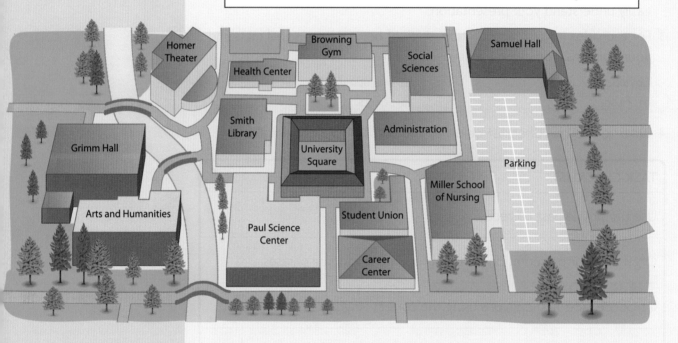

WHILE LISTENING

2 ▶ 1.8 Listen to the campus tour. Circle on the map the six places mentioned and write them in column A.

A Place	B What students can do there
Administration building	pay tuition

3 ▶ 1.8 Listen again and complete column B in the table.

Get to know your campus. Make sure that you understand what resources and services are available and where you can find them.

PRACTICE

4 Work in small groups. Which of the following can you do at or near your school? Check the boxes. Say where you can do this.

	no	I'm not sure	yes	Where?
1 park				
2 take public transportation				
3 pay tuition				
4 buy books				
5 get a snack				
6 find out about jobs				
7 find out about social events				
8 get academic help				
9 get computer help				
10 study in a quiet place				
11 meet with a teacher or professor				

5 Discuss the questions.

1 What services and resources are the most important to have at a school? Why?
2 What is your favorite place to study? Describe it and say why you like to study there.

REAL-WORLD APPLICATION

6 Work in small groups. Plan a tour for visitors to your school. Use a map, if one is available.

1 Think of five places to visit.
2 Choose a good route. Where would the tour begin and end?
3 Plan what you would say about each place. Include information about what you can do there, when the place is open, and why the place is important.

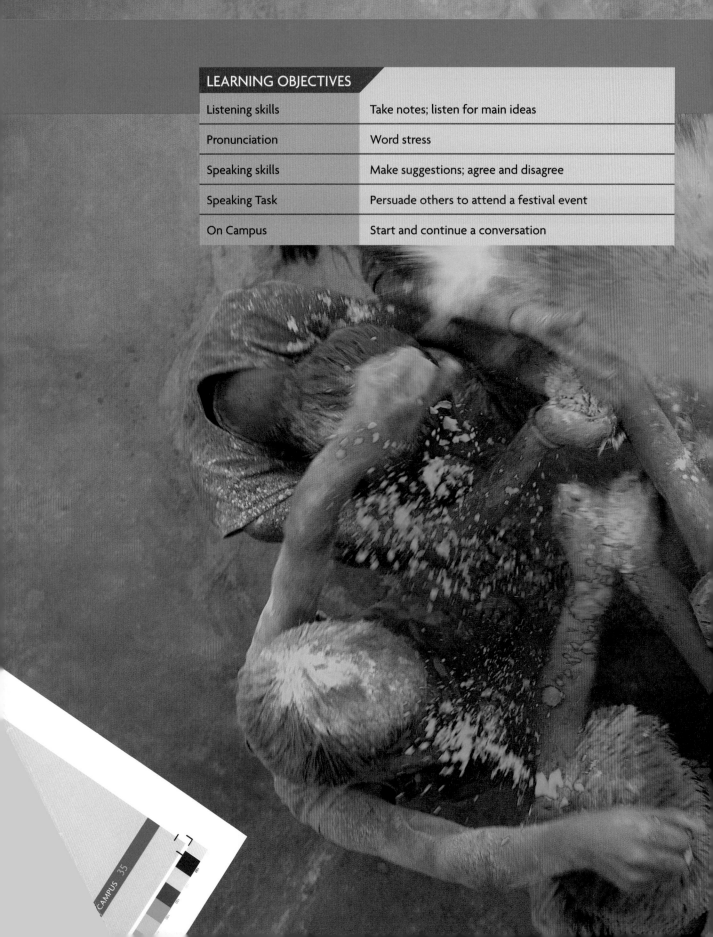

Listening skills	Take notes; listen for main ideas
Pronunciation	Word stress
Speaking skills	Make suggestions; agree and disagree
Speaking Task	Persuade others to attend a festival event
On Campus	Start and continue a conversation

FESTIVALS AND CELEBRATIONS

ACTIVATE YOUR KNOWLEDGE

Work with a partner. Look at the photo and answer the questions.

1 Which country do you think the festival is held in?

2 Are there any public festivals in your country that use color?

3 A public festival is for everyone, but a private celebration is only for family and friends. What kinds of festivals and celebrations have you been to?

PREPARING TO WATCH

ACTIVATING YOUR
KNOWLEDGE

1 Work with a partner and answer the questions.

1 What are the coldest countries in the world?
2 What do people do there during the winter?
3 How do people in your country use ice? What do they use it for?

PREDICTING CONTENT

2 You are going to watch a video about an ice festival in Harbin, China. Make a list of things you think you will see in the video. Compare your answers with a partner.

GLOSSARY

bitter (adj) very cold

Boeing 747 (n) a type of large airplane

certain (adj) if something is certain, we are sure about it

melt (v) if something melts, it changes from solid to liquid because of heat

spectacle (n) an unusual event that attracts attention or interest

thaw (n) a period of warmer weather that melts ice and snow

WHILE WATCHING

UNDERSTANDING
DETAILS

3 ▶ Watch the video. Then circle the correct answers.

1 Harbin is called an ice *town / city*.
2 Harbin has an ice festival every *year / two years*.
3 The average temperature in Harbin is *7°F / 11°F* in the winter.
4 *Four / Seven* thousand people worked to put the festival together.
5 They used enough ice and snow to fill nearly *20 / 200* Boeing 747s.
6 This ice festival begins on *January / February* 5.

4 ▶ Watch the video again and correct the student's notes.

- Siberian temperatures are bitter in the summer.
- People build a big ice city.
- The city is built out of ice and sand.
- More than one thousand visitors are expected to come.
- There are water slides.
- The end date is certain.

5 Match the questions to the answers.

  1 Why do organizers hope there's no thaw? _____
  2 Why is Harbin a good place for an ice festival? _____
  3 Why is the end date of the festival not certain? _____
  4 Why do people go to the ice festival? _____

  a It's bitter cold.
  b It's a spectacle.
  c They don't want the ice to melt.
  d It depends on the temperature.

DISCUSSION

6 Work in small groups. Discuss your answers.

  1 Would you like to go to Harbin's ice festival? Why or why not?
  2 Do you think the ice festival is important to Harbin? Explain
    your answer.
  3 Describe a winter festival in your town, city, or country.

7 Imagine you are going to Harbin's ice festival. Make a list of five to eight
  things to take with you. Compare your answers with other groups.

LISTENING

LISTENING 1

PREPARING TO LISTEN

UNDERSTANDING
KEY VOCABULARY

1 You are going to listen to some interviews about three festivals. Read the sentences. Choose the correct definition for the word in bold.

1 We listened and took notes while the professor gave the **lecture**.
   a book about a subject
   b formal talk given to a group of people to teach them about a subject

2 There were many **activities** at the festival, like watching shows or playing games.
   a things you do for fun
   b exams or tests

3 Celebrating holidays with a big meal is **traditional** in many countries.
   a part of older ways of doing things and older ideas that are not modern
   b modern

4 If a festival is about **culture**, tourists often enjoy going to it because they can learn about the way of life of the local community.
   a the habits and traditions of a country or group of people
   b work and business of a country

5 We enjoyed listening to the **band** because they played and sang well.
   a type of music
   b group of musicians who play music together

6 A popular type of **entertainment** at a festival is watching a race or competition.
   a shows, movies, games, or other ways of having fun
   b classes, lectures, or other ways of learning

7 We **enjoyed** the delicious food.
   a got pleasure from
   b did something with someone

2 List the words in bold from Exercise 1 below the photos that they can describe. In some items, more than one answer is possible.

a   b   c

_____   _____   _____

3 Match the festivals to the photos in Exercise 2.

   1 The Cambridge Festival of Ideas _____
   2 The Muscat Festival _____
   3 Iceland Airwaves Music Festival _____

4 Work with a partner. Use the photos and the names of the festivals to predict what types of things you can do at each festival.

WHILE LISTENING

Taking notes

Taking notes helps you organize and remember information. Focus on main points and important details. Remember that notes should be short. If you write too much, you sometimes miss the next part of the listening. Only write the most important words.

Place: ~~the festival is in~~ Muscat

5 Before you listen, practice keeping your notes short. Cross out the words that are not needed in the notes.

   1 Date: The festival is in April and May.
   2 Activities: You can see art, and you can try cooking.

6 ▶ **2.1** Listen to the interviews. Take notes to complete the tourist information in the festival brochures.

THE CAMBRIDGE FESTIVAL OF IDEAS

Place: Cambridge, (1)_____
Month: (2)_____
Activities: study (3)_____ : English Civil War (1642–1651)
learn about science: play games to learn about (4)_____
listen to a (5)_____ on the economy

ICELAND AIRWAVES MUSIC FESTIVAL

Place: Reykjavik, Iceland
Month: (6)_____
Activities: listen to (7)_____ by international bands
go to clubs, visit natural places, and visit (8)_____

THE MUSCAT FESTIVAL OF HERITAGE AND CULTURE

Place: Muscat, Oman
Months: (9)_____ and (10)_____
Activities: (11)_____ : cycling, camel race
learn traditional (12)_____
go to a (13)_____ show
eat traditional food

7 ▶ **2.1** Listen again. Write *T* (true) or *F* (false) next to the statements. Then correct the false statements.

_____ 1 The Festival of Ideas is only for students.
_____

_____ 2 Both kids and adults enjoy going to the Festival of Ideas.
_____

_____ 3 At the Iceland Airwaves festival, only bands from Iceland play.
_____

_____ 4 Organizers started holding the Iceland Airwaves festival in 2009.
_____

_____ 5 People can learn about Oman's culture at the Muscat Festival.
_____

_____ 6 Nasrra was able to go to a fashion show at the Muscat Festival.
_____

DISCUSSION

8 Work with a partner. Use your notes from Exercise 6 to choose the most interesting festival and which activities you would like to do most.

9 Talk to at least three other people in the class. Discuss the festival and the activities you each chose.

10 Compare your answers with the rest of the class. Which festivals and activities are most popular?

PRONUNCIATION FOR LISTENING

Word stress

Speakers often stress words that are important for listeners to understand. Different stress in a sentence can have different meanings.

I want to go to the fashion show.

In the example above, if the speaker stresses *I*, then the important information is *who* wants to go to the fashion show.

If the speaker stresses *the fashion show*, then *the event* is the important information.

11 Look at the sentence from Listening 1. Which words are important for understanding the sentence? Underline them.

> Well, it's an interesting event to come to.

PRISM Online Workbook

12 2.2 Listen to the sentence from Exercise 11. Which words are stressed?

13 Look at the questions from the listening. Underline the stressed words.

1 So, what kinds of things do people learn?
2 Are there any things you don't like about it?
3 Do you have many people here from other countries?

14 2.3 Listen and check. Repeat the questions.

15 Read the questions about free time. Underline the important words.

    1 What activities do you do in your free time?
    2 Do you have any hobbies?
    3 What did you do last weekend?

16 Work with a partner. Ask and answer the questions using correct stress.

⊙ LANGUAGE DEVELOPMENT

GERUNDS AND INFINITIVES

When you learn a new verb, it is important to learn the structures that can follow it. When two verbs come together, the second verb is usually an infinitive (*to* + the base form of a verb) or a gerund (the base form of a verb + *-ing*).

We **want to go** to the ice festival this winter.
I **enjoy learning** about other cultures.

verbs followed by an infinitive	verbs followed by a gerund	verbs followed by an infinitive or a gerund
decide	enjoy	begin
hope	finish	continue
learn	keep	hate
need	stop	like
plan		love
want		prefer
		start

1 Circle the correct form of the verbs in the sentences. Sometimes both are correct.

1 I enjoy *to learn / learning* about all the new ideas ...
2 In 1999 organizers started *to hold / holding* this festival every year in Reykjavik, the capital of Iceland.
3 Some people prefer *to visit / visiting* Reykjavik's many museums.
4 My mother and father want *to watch / watching* some of the sports ...
5 But I decided *to go / going* to the fashion show.
6 After we finish *to watch / watching* the races and shows, we'll go and eat some traditional food.
7 I plan *to visit / visiting* Iceland Airwaves next fall.
8 The festival organizers began *to sell / selling* tickets to the festival on Friday morning.

2 Write the infinitive or gerund form of the verb to complete the sentences. In some items, than one answer is possible.

1 I started _____ (learn) languages because I'm very interested in traveling.
2 She wanted _____ (go) to the festival in Iceland.
3 I prefer _____ (attend) sports events rather than look at art.
4 He decided _____ (go) on a vacation to Iceland so that he could attend the music festival.
5 What time will the presenter finish _____ (talk) about gravity?
6 I enjoy _____ (go) to festivals because it's a great way to learn about local culture.
7 I hope _____ (visit) Iceland next year.
8 I really like _____ (go) to food festivals. They always have some really interesting food.
9 The organization will continue _____ (invite) important people to the festival.

3 Work with a partner. Check your answers.

COLLOCATIONS

A collocation is a combination of two or more words that are often used together.

go to college, go to a talk, go to class

PRISM Online Workbook

4 Label each circle with the correct words from the box to make verb + noun collocations. Some words can be used more than once.

> a celebration (x2)   care   college   a concert   an event (x2)
> a festival   fun   a good time   a lecture   a party (x2)
> part   place   a photo   a problem   a video   your time

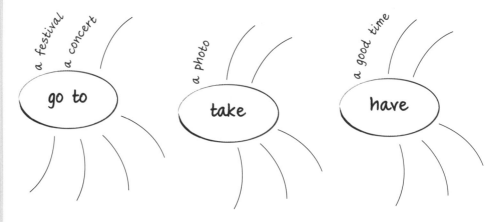

5 Write the correct form of *go to*, *have*, or *take*.

1 Excuse me, can you _____ a photo of my sister and me?
2 What time will you leave your house to _____ the celebration?
3 I'm going on vacation next week. Will you _____ care of my plants?
4 _____ a good time on your vacation!
5 I'm sorry that I can't go to your party tonight. But I hope you _____ fun!

6 Write the correct form of the words from Exercise 4. In some items, more than one answer is possible.

1 What do you think makes a good festival? Should everyone go to every _____ , or is it OK to miss some of them?
2 Do you take _____ to enjoy a festival when you go, or do you hurry to see things?
3 In your country do people often go to _____ to listen to music?
4 If it's your birthday, do you have a _____ ?

7 Work with a partner. Ask and answer the questions.

PREPARING TO LISTEN

UNDERSTANDING
KEY VOCABULARY

PRISM Online
Workbook

1 You are going to listen to a discussion about a holiday. Read the sentences. Write the words in bold next to the definitions.

1 We are planning a party to **celebrate** my mother's 80th birthday.
2 The actors wore gorilla **costumes** in the movie.
3 A traditional U.S. Thanksgiving **dish** is candied sweet potatoes. It is made with sweet potatoes, brown sugar, and butter.
4 The baker **decorated** the cake with colorful flowers made of sugar.
5 I love colorful **fireworks**, but the loud sound scares my dog.
6 In the U.S. many people give small **gifts** to their friends on their birthdays, like a book or a small box of chocolates.
7 Every year there is a big **parade** on Thanksgiving. People march down the street with giant balloons and play music.

a _____ (n) one type of food prepared as part of a bigger meal

b _____ (n) small objects that explode to make a loud noise and bright colors, and are often used for special events

c _____ (n) a line of people or vehicles that moves through the street to celebrate a special day or event

d _____ (v) to do something fun because it is a special day or because something good has happened

e _____ (n) something special that you give to someone else

f _____ (n) clothes that people wear to make them look like someone or something else

g _____ (v) to make something look pretty by putting things on it

2 Look at the photos. Which words from Exercise 1 can you match to the photos? In some items, more than one answer is possible.

_____ _____ _____ _____

3 Work with a partner. Which types of celebrations or holidays are related to these photos?

PREDICTING CONTENT
USING VISUALS

SKILLS

Listening for main ideas

Main ideas are the most important ideas about the topic being discussed. To help you figure out what the main idea is, think about the topic. What about the topic does the speaker focus on? For example, a main idea about the topic of festivals could be that they have a lot of fun activities. So that is what the speaker or writer talks about. Take notes on the main ideas as you listen.

TAKING NOTES ON MAIN IDEAS

PRISM Online Workbook

4 ▶ 2.4 Listen to the discussion. Write the main ideas. Remember that main ideas are the most important ideas about a topic.

North American holiday: (1)_____
U.S. & Canada celebrate – everyone thankful
(2)_____ and friends – eat meal together
(3)_____ meal: turkey, stuffing, potatoes, corn, cranberries, pie

(4)_____ differences:

(5)_____	(6)_____
(7)_____ : spicy	sweet, whipped cream
(8)_____ : rice or bread	cornbread, oysters

(9)_____ : leaves, fall vegetables, candles
(10)_____ (red, yellow, orange)

Canadian Thanksgiving: October; American Thanksgiving: November

(11)_____ : parades, watch TV, sports; no gifts

(12)_____ : small local parade, (13)_____ : big New York City parade on TV

(14) Different _____ for the holiday
Canada: fall harvest
U.S.: fall harvest + remembering Native Americans helping settlers hunt and grow food

5 ▶ **2.4** Listen again. Write *T* (true) or *F* (false) next to the statements. Then correct the false statements.

LISTENING FOR DETAILS

_____ 1 In New York City, the Thanksgiving parade is very huge.
_____

_____ 2 In the southern U.S., sometimes oysters are used for stuffing.
_____

_____ 3 Canadian turkey stuffing is often made from cornbread.
_____

_____ 4 People usually eat spicy pumpkin pie for Canadian Thanksgiving.
_____

_____ 5 Potatoes, corn, and cranberries are traditional foods from Europe.
_____

POST-LISTENING

6 ▶ **2.5** Listen to the examples related to Thanksgiving. Complete the sentences with phrases for introducing examples.

RECOGNIZING EXAMPLES

1 ... some people prefer different kinds of pie, _____ apple.
2 ... people often decorate their dinner tables and homes with things _____ colorful leaves, fall vegetables, and candles.
3 _____ , both countries celebrate with parades with marching bands and people in costumes.
4 In Canada, _____ , the holiday is celebrated on the second Monday in October.

7 Look at each phrase in Exercise 6 and answer the questions.

1 Which two ways of introducing examples can be followed by a noun?
_____ , _____

2 Which two ways of introducing examples can be followed by a subject and a verb or by a comma and a noun? _____ , _____

DISCUSSION

8 Work with a partner. Choose two of the festivals and celebrations from Listening 1 and Listening 2. Fill in the table with what you think are positive and negative parts of each. Share your opinions with your partner.

SYNTHESIZING

festival	positive	negative

SPEAKING

CRITICAL THINKING

At the end of this unit, you are going to do the Speaking Task below.

> Choose a group of events from a festival and persuade your group to go to them.

1 Read the website about the Winter Carnival in Minnesota. Find one group of events you would like to attend.

Winter Carnival Parades

If you love parades, the Winter Carnival has three! The nighttime Moon Glow Parade has hot chocolate and treats. Marchers carry colorful glowing lights. Or how about watching the king of winter, King Boreas, as he comes to town with marching bands, floats, and people in costumes? And don't miss the last parade with the lively Vulcan Krewe. They fight for warm weather, marching through town to battle King Boreas so the cold weather will go away. Celebrate their win with fantastic fireworks!

Competitions and Races

Do you like competitions and sports? Why not watch college teams compete to build robots to clean the snow? Or you can join the competitions for snow or ice sculpture to win prizes. You could also run a race through the city with thousands of people. How about watching ice skaters race down a hill? Or watch the bouncing teams use a blanket to bounce people high into the air? See who bounces the highest!

Buried Treasures

Are you good at puzzles? Do you want to find treasure? Be sure to read the newspaper for clues to find a $10,000 prize hidden in the city snow. Sometimes it takes two weeks with hundreds of people looking to find the prize. Kids should try the children's treasure hunt at the snow park for candy and coins.

Snow and Ice Events

At the Snow Park, you can see snow sculptures, slide down a giant snow slide, or make giant snow walls. How about going ice skating at the ice palace? Why not take a photo with the blue-costumed King Boreas and his royal family? Or take a ride on a fire truck with the Vulcan Krewe, the red-costumed group that fights for warm weather.

Organizing ideas

Use a table to organize ideas about a complicated topic. Only write words and short phrases (not sentences) in each section to quickly record a lot of information about the topic before you start speaking.

2 Work with a partner. Write notes about possible positives and negatives for each of the events described in the text.

EVALUATE ▲

events	ideas	
	positives	negatives
parades	hot chocolate and treats	very crowded
competitions and races		
buried treasures		
snow and ice events		

3 Look at the poster for the Winter Carnival. This poster tries to persuade people to come to the events. What things in this poster help you decide if you want to go or not?

WINTER CARNIVAL

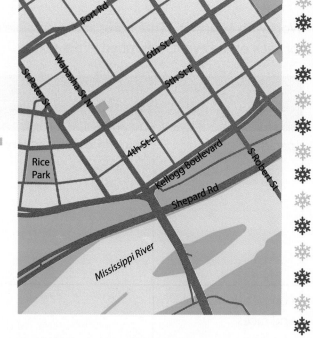

When and Where?

Location: St. Paul, Minnesota

Time of year: January

Plan your visit now!

History of the Festival

This ten-day festival began in 1886 and offers more than 100 events, including parades, races, competitions, and buried treasure!

Ice Palaces and Snow Parks

Walk through the amazing ice palace. See the ice-carving displays. Go ice skating or slide on the giant snow slide. Feel chilly? Warm up with hot chocolate or a seat by the fire. How about coming inside to listen to the symphony or have a wonderful meal? It's all part of the festival. Come join King Boreas, king of winter, as he celebrates his season in Minnesota.

Enjoy the Battle of Winter and Spring

Watch for King Boreas and his court dressed in blue, as they entertain the city with races, parades, music, and shows. But look out for the wild and crazy Vulcan Krewe wearing red and riding a fire truck. Will King Boreas win this year? Or will the Vulcan Krewe win again and chase winter away from the city? Don't miss their battle at the ice palace after the last parade on the last night of the festival. Amazing fireworks will celebrate the winner!

MAKING SUGGESTIONS

> **SKILLS**
>
> We make suggestions when we give advice to someone. We also make suggestions when we are deciding what to do with someone.
>
> Visitors **should try** to go to the cake shop.
> **Why not** try this activity?
> **How about** driving to the festival?

1 Put the words in order to make suggestions.

1 should / try / You / it /.

_____

2 starting / How / cake / ? / with / about

_____

3 not / Why / yourself / ? / try it

_____

2 Check (✔) the sentences and questions that make suggestions.

1 I will try that. ☐
2 How about trying this? ☐
3 Can I try? ☐
4 I'd suggest trying this. ☐
5 Should we try this? ☐
6 Can we think about trying this? ☐

3 Complete the table with the suggestion sentences and questions from Exercises 1 and 2.

infinitive without *to*	gerund
1 _____ .	4 _____ ?
2 _____ ?	5 _____ .
3 _____ ?	6 _____ ?

4 Complete the dialogue with the suggestion sentences and questions from Exercise 3. Try not to use the same expression more than once.

Man: This festival is fantastic. What do you want to do first?

Woman: (1)_____ we go to the food tent? I'd like to get some pizza.

Man: OK. Good idea. After that (2)_____ visiting the art exhibition? I'd like to see some of the paintings.

Woman: Yeah, that sounds good. Then we (3)_____ go and do a singing workshop.

Man: Oh, I'm not sure that's a good idea. I'm a terrible singer!

Woman: OK, well (4)_____ listening to the talk on poetry instead?

Man: Yeah, I'd love to! That's a great idea!

Woman: What (5)_____ we do after that?

Man: Well, by then we will probably need to go home!

Woman: Hmm, I might want to see other things. How about we look at the gift shop after?

Man: Sure! That sounds good.

5 Work with a partner. Read the dialogue aloud. Did you choose the same phrases?

AGREEING AND DISAGREEING

When responding to suggestions it is important to be polite, whether you agree or disagree with the suggestion. When people reply with *yes*, it is rarely on its own. When people reply with *no*, they often add other words to make the meaning softer.

Yes: That's a great idea!   **No:** I'm not sure that's a good idea.

6 Look at the dialogue in Exercise 4. Underline the two ways to say "no" and highlight the five ways to say "yes" to the suggestions.

SPEAKING TASK

PRISM Online Workbook

Choose a group of events from a festival and persuade your group to go to them.

PREPARE

1 Look at the events in Exercise 1 and your table in Exercise 2 in Critical Thinking. Add any new information to your table.

2 Decide with your partner which group of events you will go to. You will try to persuade another pair to go to those events.

3 Think of some phrases you can use to make suggestions about which event to go to. You can use language like this:

How about ...   Why don't we try ...   We should ...

4 Complete the notes to help you prepare for your discussion.

Our event is _____ [write the type of event].
It takes place in _____ [place] in _____ [month].
At the event you can _____ [activities].
You can (eat / drink / see / hear) _____ .

5 Refer to the Task Checklist below as you prepare for your discussion.

TASK CHECKLIST	✔
Use basic verb patterns correctly.	
Use vocabulary and collocations from this unit.	
Make suggestions.	
Agree or disagree using appropriate language.	
Come to a final decision as a group.	

DISCUSS

6 With your partner, work with another pair who chose a different event. Each pair should:

- describe the event and the activities.
- make suggestions about what to do and why it would be fun.

The other pair will try to persuade you to go to their events. As you listen to the other pair, you should:

- ask questions about the event.
- use appropriate language to show that you agree or disagree.

7 As a group, choose an event that everyone would like to go to.

8 As a group, tell the class which event you chose and why.

ON CAMPUS

STARTING AND CONTINUING A CONVERSATION

PREPARING TO LISTEN

1 You are going to listen to people starting conversations. Before you listen, work with a partner. Discuss the questions.

   1 When and where do you meet English-speaking people?
   2 How do you feel about starting conversations in English?
   3 What kinds of things do people usually ask you?
   4 What topics do people discuss when they meet for the first time?

WHILE LISTENING

2 ▶ 2.6 Listen to the conversations. Circle the topics that you hear. What do the students in each conversation have in common?

Conversation 1
home town/country   transportation   weather   classes   sports
Conversation 2
home town/country   transportation   weather   classes   sports

SKILLS

When you meet someone for the first time, try to find a topic that interests you both. This allows the conversation to continue.

• Choose topics that you might have in common: the weather, transportation, school, classes, where you are from, sports, entertainment, or music.
• Ask questions with words like *what, where, when,* and *how,* so that your partner can say more.

3 ▶ 2.6 Listen again. Complete the excerpts.

Conversation 1
1 How long have you been in the U.S.?
  About a year. _____ ? Where are you from?
2 It's very different from here.
  Really? _____ ?
3 What's your major?
  I'm not sure yet. Maybe business management.
  Oh, me too! _____ ?

Conversation 2

4 I've been in the U.S. for three years. But this is my first year here.
   _____ so far?

5 Actually, I have an apartment off campus.
   Oh! _____ ?

PRACTICE

4 Answer these questions. Then add information or ask a question to continue the conversation.

   1 Where are you from?
     I'm from Shanghai, China. What about you?

   2 What kind of food do you like?
     _____

   3 What do you usually do on weekends?
     _____

   4 How do you get to school?
     _____

   5 How do you like living here?
     _____

5 Work with a partner. Take turns asking and answering the questions. Try to continue the conversations.

REAL-WORLD APPLICATION

6 Choose one of the topics. Write three to five questions that you could ask about the topic.

school and classes	free-time activities or holidays
home country and language	weather
sports and exercise	

What's your city / major / favorite sports team?

Do you live / like / play ... ?

How do you like ... ?

Are you interested in ... ?

What's that like?

7 Stand up and introduce yourself to another student. Think of a topic that might interest him or her. Try to continue the conversation.

8 After a few minutes, say *It was nice to meet you.* Then introduce yourself to another student and repeat the exercise.

LEARNING OBJECTIVES

Listening skill	Listen for reasons
Pronunciation	Consonant sounds /s/, /ʃ/, /tʃ/; strong /æ/ and weak /ə/
Speaking skill	Give additional and contrasting information
Speaking Task	Present a report about a device or technology
On Campus	Technology for learning

ACTIVATE YOUR KNOWLEDGE

Work with a partner. Look at the photo and answer the questions.

1 What kind of technology do you use every day at home, at school, or at work?

2 Which kind of technology would be difficult to live without?

3 What are some examples of technology used in medicine, communication, and entertainment?

4 Do you think there are disadvantages to technology? What are they?

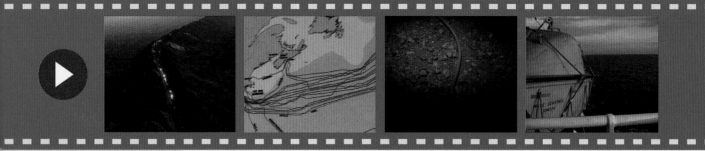

PREPARING TO WATCH

ACTIVATING YOUR KNOWLEDGE

1 Work with a partner and answer the questions.

1 Do you mainly use the Internet on your cell phone, a tablet, or a computer? Why?
2 Did you ever need the Internet, but it didn't work? Why didn't it work?
3 What do people and businesses do when there is no Internet?

PREDICTING CONTENT USING VISUALS

2 Look at the pictures from the video and answer the questions.

1 What problem do you think you will see in the video?
2 How do you think they will solve the problem?

GLOSSARY

crash (v) to stop working suddenly and sometimes violently

fiber optic cables (n) very thin glass or plastic wires that carry information in phones, televisions, and computer systems

go dead (phr v) to stop working

violent (adj) sudden and causing damage

volcanic (adj) related to a volcano

WHILE WATCHING

UNDERSTANDING MAIN IDEAS

3 ▶ Watch the video and circle the correct answer. Compare your answers with a partner.

1 Volcanic activity *doesn't change* / *changes* the ocean floor.
2 Internet traffic goes through cables at the *top* / *bottom* of the ocean.
3 *Most* / *Some* of the Internet traffic goes through cables in the ocean.
4 Cables *slowly* / *suddenly* went dead.
5 *Scientists* / *Engineers* looked for the problem.
6 They found the cables were *broken* / *fixed*.
7 It took *days* / *weeks* to find and repair the cables.
8 A special kind of *ship* / *plane* helps keep the Internet connected.

4 ▶ Watch again. Put the sentences in the order you hear them (1–5).

a Computers all over Asia crashed. _____
b It took time to find and repair the cables. _____
c They looked for the problem. _____
d Important fiber optic cables went dead. _____
e Many people couldn't use the Internet. _____

UNDERSTANDING DETAILS

5 Work with a partner and answer the questions.

1 What kind of activity happened in the middle of the ocean?
2 When did the important fiber optic cables go dead?
3 Where did the fiber optic cables go dead?
4 What moved at the bottom of the ocean and broke the cables?
5 What did they use to find and repair the cables?

6 The speaker in the video asks, "What would happen to businesses?" What do you think would happen? Circle the answer(s) that you think are possible.

a People would stop working.
b Businesses would find other ways to do business.
c Businesses would shut down.

MAKING INFERENCES

DISCUSSION

7 Work with a partner. Discuss the questions.

1 What are some ways that people use the Internet?
2 How did people do these things before the Internet?
3 Do you think the Internet will be different in 20 years? If so, how?

8 Work in small groups. Think about what happens when technology stops working. Complete the statements. Then share your answers with another group.

1 When cable TV stops working, people can …
2 When traffic lights stop working, drivers can …
3 When telephones stop working, businesses can …
4 When electric trains and subways stop working, passengers can …

LISTENING

LISTENING 1

UNDERSTANDING KEY VOCABULARY

PREPARING TO LISTEN

1 You are going to listen to a student radio program about robots. Read the sentences. Choose the correct definition for the word in bold.

1 Nathan made a mistake while driving, had an **accident**, and crashed his car.
   a something bad that happens that is not on purpose and that causes injury or damage
   b something that happens that is a secret

2 The scientist **collected** water from the ocean and tested it in a lab. She found out that the water was very polluted.
   a forgot something
   b got things from different places and brought them together

3 The company **developed** a new mini-robot for house cleaning last year. Everyone was excited to buy it.
   a tried something
   b made something new

4 After the car crash, Frank was **disabled** and couldn't walk anymore.
   a having an illness or injury that makes it difficult to do the things that other people do
   b not knowing how to do something

5 Some people think that taking a long vacation is a **luxury**. They don't have enough time or money to really enjoy one.
   a something expensive that you enjoy but do not need
   b something that you have never done before

6 Nowadays, **robots** are used by doctors to do surgery.
   a information that people study
   b machines controlled by a computer that can move and do other things that people can do

7 People often wear a **suit** when they go for a job interview so they will look professional.
   a an outfit of T-shirt and jeans
   b an outfit of a jacket and pants or a jacket and skirt that are made from the same material

8 The student needed to find **information** about how cities clean up pollution. He looked online, found books in the library, and read academic papers about the subject.
   a objects used to do scientific experiments
   b facts about a situation, person, event, etc.

2 Discuss the questions in pairs.

    1 What are some things that robots can do nowadays?

    2 What does a robot look like?

3 What do you see in each photo?

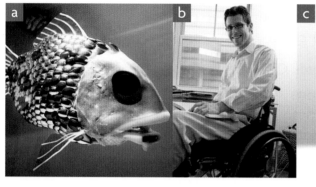

a   b   c   d   e

_____ _____ _____ _____ _____

4 Match the words from the box to the photos in Exercise 3.

> di_s_abled   fi_sh_   ki_tch_en   _s_uit   pollu_ti_on

PRONUNCIATION FOR LISTENING

SKILLS

Consonant sounds /s/, /ʃ/, /tʃ/

The consonant sounds /s/ _subject_, /ʃ/ _show_, /tʃ/ _teacher_ are easily confused.
It is important to listen closely for these different sounds.

/s/ _save_   /ʃ/ _shave_
/tʃ/ _watch_   /ʃ/ _wash_

5 ▶ 3.1 Listen to the words from Exercise 4 and the explanation box. Pay attention to the underlined sounds.

6 Work with a partner. Say the words in Exercise 4 aloud and pay attention to the underlined sound. Add each word to the sound maps.

PRISM Online Workbook

subject

/s/

show

/ʃ/

teacher

/tʃ/

7 ▶ **3.2** Listen to the words. Add the words to the sound maps in Exercise 6.

1 sta<u>t</u>ion
2 <u>s</u>ort
3 <u>sh</u>ort
4 wi<u>sh</u>
5 whi<u>ch</u>

6 robot<u>s</u>
7 ma<u>tch</u>
8 o<u>c</u>ean
9 ac<u>c</u>ident
10 <u>ch</u>eap

8 ▶ **3.3** Listen to the words. Circle the word you hear.

1 shorts   sorts
2 sheep   cheap
3 wash   watch
4 sea   she
5 save   shave

9 Work with a partner. Predict the answers to the questions. What else do you think robots can do?

1 What sorts of robots are there?
2 Do you think robots are cheap or expensive?
3 Can robots wash clothes?
4 Can robots measure pollution in the ocean?
5 Can robots help a disabled person shave?

TAKING NOTES ON
MAIN IDEAS

WHILE LISTENING

10 ▶ **3.4** Listen to the radio program. Complete the student's notes.

Types of (1)_____ : industrial, waiter, teacher
Robots are (2)_____ now than in past, not expensive
Medical Robot
Helps (3)_____ people walk after (4)_____ :
robotic (5)_____
Service Robot
Saves time: does boring/dirty work, e.g., wash and clean
Elderly people can stay (6)_____ longer – important,
not a (7)_____
Research Robot
Assists scientists with (8)_____ : robot fish
Scientists can (9)_____ ocean pollution quickly

11 Use your notes to check your predictions from Exercise 9.

Listening for reasons

People often talk about reasons for things happening.

I passed my exam **because** *I worked hard. Working hard is the reason I passed my exam.*

When people give reasons for things, they use words like *since, because of, thanks to,* and *due to.* If you hear these you know a reason will follow.

12 ▶ 3.4 Listen again. Write the missing information to complete the table.

PRISM Online Workbook

event	reason
Robots were not used very much in the past	... **since** robots were (1)_____ .
People have a much better quality of life	... **thanks to** these (2)_____ .
Joey Abbica couldn't walk	... **because of** an (3)_____ .
Scientists can find out about pollution quickly	... **due to** the (4)_____ .

POST-LISTENING

13 Write the words from the box to complete the sentences. In some items, more than one answer is possible.

because of   due to   since   thanks to

1 _____ Wi-Fi, Julie was able to do her work on her tablet in a café.
2 Mark couldn't use his laptop _____ a problem with the hard drive.
3 His laptop broke _____ he was careless and dropped it.
4 _____ a bad Internet connection, Bill wasn't able to email me.

DISCUSSION

14 Work with a partner and answer the questions.

1 In what ways have robots changed society?
2 Are robots good or bad? Give reasons for your answer.
3 Are there jobs or tasks that only people are able to do?
   Why or why not?
4 Are there jobs or tasks that could be done completely by robots?
   Why or why not?

CAN / BE ABLE TO

LANGUAGE

Statements

Can (+), can't (–), and be able to (+) / be not able to (–) are used to talk about general ability in the present.

Robots **can / are able to** help people in their everyday lives.
She **can't / isn't able to** do housework easily.

Could (+) and couldn't (–) are used to talk about general ability in the past.

Before the accident, Joey **could** surf really well.
After the accident, he **couldn't** walk at all.

Was/Were able to (+), wasn't/weren't able to (–), and couldn't (–) are used to talk about a specific event or a specific action in the past. Could is not used in this way.

He **wasn't** even **able to** sit up on his own when a visitor came.
He **was able to** stand up when he finally put on the robotic suit.
He **couldn't** feel his legs when doctors touched them.

Questions

Present: **Can you / Are you able to** swim?

Past: **Could you / Were you able to** speak when you were two years old?

PRISM Online Workbook

1 Read the paragraph. Complete the sentences with the correct form of can, could, or be able to.

Robots today (1)_____ (be able to +) work in many jobs faster and easier than people (2)_____ (can +). For example, robots (3)_____ (can +) put online orders together for customers. They (4)_____ (can +) handle more than 300 items in an hour. In the past, people (5)_____ (be able to –) do work as fast as robots can now. When robots were first invented, they (6)_____ (could +) only do a single job at a time. Nowadays, many robots (7)_____ (can +) perform multiple jobs at once. But don't worry; robots (8)_____ (be able to –) take all the jobs. There are some things robots (9)_____ (can –) do. For example, a robot (10)_____ (can +) cook a meal, but only a chef (11)_____ (be able to +) create a tasty new dish. Also, robots (12)_____ (be able to –) surprise their developers; they (13)_____ (can +) only do what they are built to do. But in the future, robots will probably (14)_____ (be able to +) carry out tasks that we (15)_____ (can –) even imagine today.

2 In each box, write one activity that you might do during your week.

1 finish my homework	2 play the guitar	3
4	5	6
7	8	9

3 Work with a partner. Take turns asking about each other's ability to do the activities you wrote in Exercise 2 using the past or present. Give reasons for your answers.

Student A: Were you able to finish your homework last night?
Student B: Yeah. I did it right away after school, so I had enough time.

VOCABULARY FOR TECHNOLOGY

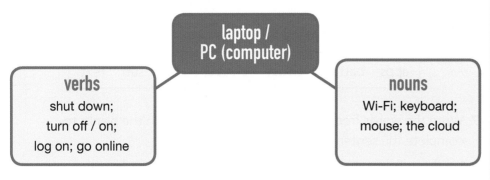

4 Write technology words from the word map to complete the sentences. Use a dictionary to help you.

1 My laptop is getting old; when I _____ it _____ , it takes a long time to start.
2 I like my touchscreen computer. Now I don't need to use the _____ to move the cursor around.
3 I can't _____ to my email because I forgot my password.
4 Do you have _____ ? I'd like to _____ and check Facebook™.
5 I finished my essay. I could send it by email or upload it to _____ so you can download it to your computer.
6 Don't forget to _____ the laptop when you finish your essay.

PRISM Online Workbook

5 Work with a partner. Answer the questions.

1 Why is it important to have a good password? Should people use more than one password for different sites?

2 Where do you prefer to save most of your files and other important electronic information? Why?

3 How often do you use Wi-Fi?

4 What do you usually spend your time doing online?

6 Put the words from the box into the correct place on the word map. One of the words is both a verb and a noun.

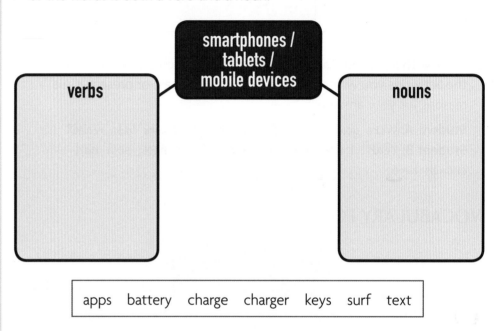

```
          smartphones /
            tablets /
         mobile devices

  verbs                    nouns
```

| apps | battery | charge | charger | keys | surf | text |

7 Write the words from the word map in Exercise 6 in the blanks to complete the sentences.

1 I don't like typing on a touchscreen. I prefer to type on real _____ .

2 If you have a tablet or smartphone, which are your favorite _____ and websites? Why?

3 How often do you _____ the Internet to find information? What kinds of things do you look for?

4 Do you prefer to call and talk to people or _____ them? Why?

5 Has your phone's _____ ever run out of power and stopped working at a bad time? What happened?

6 Do you take your _____ with you so you can _____ your phone at any time?

8 Work with a partner. Ask and answer the questions in Exercise 7.

PREPARING TO LISTEN

1 Work with a partner. Look at the photo and answer the questions.

1 When someone asks you a question about something that you studied in the past, do you try to remember it, or do you think about how to find the information on the Internet? Which is the better way to answer the question? Why?

2 If you want to know something, do you a) ask someone who might know, or b) look for the answer on the Internet? Why do you choose that option?

3 How could using a computer to help you find information change the way your brain works?

2 You are going to listen to a news report about how computers affect our memory. Read the sentences. Write the words in bold next to the definitions.

1 Sometimes I feel **stupid** when I can't remember something easily.
2 It is important to have a good **memory** when you are learning a new language. That way you don't forget the new words that you learn.
3 Students in college often do **research** for their upper-level science courses to learn new things about the subject.
4 Some students think that learning English is **difficult**, but others think that math is harder.
5 Sometimes it's hard to remember where you put your things. It's easy to forget the **location**.
6 The **file** was damaged, and I could not open my essay anymore. I should have made a copy.

a _____ (n) detailed study of a subject to learn more about it
b _____ (adj) silly or not intelligent
c _____ (adj) not easy; needing skill or effort to do or understand
d _____ (n) a collection of information stored in one place on a computer
e _____ (n) a place where something is found
f _____ (n) your ability to remember

PRONUNCIATION FOR LISTENING

SKILLS

Strong /æ/ and weak /ə/

Strong /æ/ and weak /ə/ are easily confused sounds. The strong sound /æ/ is always spelled with the single letter *a*.

Look at /æt/ the black /blæk/ cat /kæt/.

The weak sound /ə/ can be spelled many ways, including *a*. It is a sound that is not strongly stressed. Usually words that link information have the weak vowel sound /ə/.

I want a /ə/ peach and /ənd/ a /ə/ plum.

3 ▶ 3.5 The news reporter in the listening uses linking words to add supporting examples or details to the key information. Listen to the sentences. Underline the linking words in the sentences.

1 You will hear main ideas and additional information.
2 You will hear main ideas as well as additional information.

4 Work with a partner. Say the sentences in Exercise 3 aloud and pronounce the sounds correctly.

5 Work with a partner. Answer the questions. Think about the sounds in the linking words.

   1 Which letter do we often not say when we use *and*?
   2 Is the letter *a* in *and* strong /æ/ or weak /ə/?
   3 Is the letter *a* in the phrase *as well as* strong /æ/ or weak /ə/?

WHILE LISTENING

6 ▶ 3.6 Listen to the report. Write the missing information in the "main ideas" column of the notes.

TAKING NOTES ON MAIN IDEAS

main ideas	additional details
Scientists looked, in particular, at how computers affect our (1)_____ .	They wanted to find out if computers have changed the way we remember (6)_____ and knowledge.
What we think when we are asked (2)_____ questions has changed due to (3)_____ like Google™.	In the past, people tried to think of the (7)_____ to the question. Now people think about (8)_____ to find the answer. e.g., They think about what they might (9)_____ into Google™.
The type of (4)_____ we remember has changed.	People now forget (10)_____ , especially if they know the information will be saved on the computer. They remember the (11)_____ of the fact.
Computers are not making us stupid, but they are making us (5)_____ .	We are spending time remembering where to (12)_____ information but not on remembering the information itself.

7 ▶ 3.6 Listen again and complete the additional details in the second column of the table.

LISTENING FOR DETAILS

DISCUSSION

8 Write down one type of information you keep

a on your computer _____ .

b on your smartphone _____ .

c in the cloud _____ .

9 Compare your answers to Exercise 8 with a partner.

I keep my photos in the "Images" file on my phone and my essays in the "School" file on my laptop.

10 Discuss the questions in pairs. Use your notes from Listening 1 and Listening 2.

1 What are the possible problems with keeping information on your computer or in the cloud?

2 Do you think that robots will make people lazy about doing things in the same way computers made people lazy about remembering things? Why or why not?

3 People changed how they used their memory when it became common to look up facts on the Internet. What are some ways people could change how they use their bodies if using robots becomes part of daily life?

SPEAKING

CRITICAL THINKING

At the end of this unit, you are going to do the Speaking Task below.

> Present a report about a device or technology. Look at advantages and disadvantages, and give details to support the main ideas.

1 Look at the sentences about using computers. Decide if they are advantages (+) or disadvantages (–) and add them to the correct column in the table.

EVALUATE ▲

1 People forget facts that are stored on computers.
2 People remember where and how to find facts.
3 Computers aren't making us stupid.
4 Computers are making us lazy.
5 People aren't trying to remember information anymore.

main argument:	
Computers have changed the way we remember information.	
advantages (+)	disadvantages (–)

2 Compare your ideas with a partner. Add more advantages or disadvantages to the table.

3 Work with a partner. Choose one of the kinds of technology. Write the technology in the main argument at the top of the table. Add some advantages and disadvantages in the columns.

> Internet TV   smartphones   tablets   the cloud
> the Internet   video calling

main argument:	
Technology, such as _____ , *can affect our day-to-day lives.*	
advantages (+)	**disadvantages (–)**

4 Work with a new partner. Listen to his or her ideas. Do you have the same or different ideas?

PREPARATION FOR SPEAKING

GIVING ADDITIONAL AND CONTRASTING INFORMATION

> **SKILLS**
>
> When you link phrases and sentences that give more, or additional, information, use transition words and phrases of addition, such as *and*, *also*, *as well as*, and *too*.
>
> When you link phrases and sentences that have different, or contrasting, ideas, use transition words and phrases of contrast, such as *however*, *but*, and *on the other hand*.

1 Write the words from the box in the blanks to complete the sentences. In some items, more than one answer is possible.

> but   however   on the other hand

1 When people were asked difficult questions in the past, scientists believe they tried to think of the answer to the question. _____ , because of modern technology, the first thing people think about now is how to find the answer ...

2 For example, they think about what they might put into Google™, _____ in the past they thought about the question itself.

3 ... it seems that people now forget facts, especially if they know the information will be saved in a file. _____ , an advantage is they remember the location of the fact; in other words, where to find it.

4 In conclusion, it seems that computers are not making us stupid, _____ they are making us lazy!

2 ▶ 3.7 Listen and check. Your answers might not match the listening. Remember, some sentences have more than one possible answer. Make a note of what you hear.

3 Circle the correct option to complete the rule about the words in bold.

But, **however**, and **on the other hand** link *similar ideas / different information*.

4 Read the sentences. Do the words in bold introduce different information or additional information? _____

a People use computers to save information **and** to organize it.
b People use computers to save information **and also** to organize it.
c **Also**, people use computers to save information and to organize it.
d People use computers to save information **as well as** to organize it.
e People use computers to save information and to organize it, **too**.

5 Write the correct transition words and phrases in the sentences next to each sentence ending.

1 Computers help people look for things, *and / but*
_____ a they can find information quickly.
_____ b they can make people lazy.

2 Technology is now important for our social lives *and also / , but*
_____ a traditional activities like writing letters are disappearing.
_____ b makes it easier for us to communicate with friends.

3 Robots assist people with difficult jobs *as well as / . However,*
_____ a helping take care of elderly and disabled people.
_____ b some people believe they are bad because people lose their jobs when robots are used.

6 Read sentences *a* and *b*, and think about the function of the phrases in bold. Then circle the correct word to complete the sentence that follows.

a **To conclude**, computers are a useful way to store information, but you have to remember where you store it and how to find it again!

b **In conclusion**, computers are a useful way to store information, but you have to remember where you store it and how to find it again!

We use these expressions to *introduce / finish* what we are saying in a report.

SPEAKING TASK

Present a report about a device or technology. Look at advantages and disadvantages, and give details to support the main ideas.

PREPARE

1 Look at the advantages and disadvantages you wrote about technology in Critical Thinking. Complete these sentences with your ideas to start your report.

Today I am going to present my report on _____
(Write the name of the technology.)
The main argument I am going to present is _____
_____
(Write the main argument from your table.)

2 Write sentences about the main argument. Use language to give reasons, such as:

because of   due to   since   thanks to

3 Give additional and contrasting information. Link this information using transition words and phrases, such as:

also   and   and also   as well as   too   but   however
on the other hand

> Computers are important **because** they have changed the way we remember information. People aren't trying to remember information anymore. **Also**, they forget facts that are stored on computers, **but** they remember where and how to find facts. Computers aren't making us stupid. **However**, computers are making us lazy.

4 Add a sentence to finish what you are saying about the technology. Use language such as:

In conclusion ...   To conclude ...

5 Refer to the Task Checklist below as you prepare your presentation.

TASK CHECKLIST	✔
Use *can* and *be able to* correctly.	
Offer main ideas and supporting details using the correct language.	
Present advantages and disadvantages.	
Link sentences using transition words and phrases to contrast ideas or add extra information.	

PRACTICE

6 Practice the introduction to your report, the sentences to link advantages and disadvantages, and the conclusion.

PRESENT

7 Present your report to your partner. Discuss each of your ideas. Do you agree or disagree with your partner's ideas about technology? Why or why not?

ON CAMPUS

TECHNOLOGY FOR LEARNING

PREPARING TO LISTEN

1 Work with a partner and discuss the questions.

    1 How often do you use a computer for learning in class? Out of class?
    2 What websites and apps do you use for learning?
    3 Do you get distracted by social media while you are studying?

WHILE LISTENING

2 ▶ 3.8 You are going to hear Mandy, Feng, Erica, and Armando describe the technology they use for learning. Listen and circle the four topics that you hear.

> taking notes   sharing documents   keeping track of a schedule
>   learning vocabulary   doing research   blocking social media

3 ▶ 3.8 What do the words in bold refer to? Write the correct letter next to each excerpt. Then listen again and check your answers.

1 I take a photo of **it** and paste it into my notes.
2 I insert links so that I can find **them** again later.
3 We upload **them** to a class folder.
4 We can all work on **it** from home.
5 You can download **them** and print them out.
6 I found an app that blocks **all that stuff**.

a flashcards and quizzes
b information on the whiteboard
c papers written in class
d a presentation
e text messages and social media
f websites

PRACTICE

4 How do you use technology for learning? Complete the survey.

What apps and websites do you use to ...	I don't use technology.	I use ...
1 keep track of your schedule and due dates?		
2 do research?		
3 write papers?		
4 make graphs and charts?		
5 give presentations?		
6 share files with other students?		
7 communicate with classmates and your teacher?		
8 learn new words?		
9 take notes in class?		
10 block social media sites?		

5 Work in small groups. Compare your answers. Then discuss the questions.

    1 What websites and apps did you learn about from your classmates?

    2 What other websites and apps for learning can you recommend?

REAL-WORLD APPLICATION

6 Choose one app or website that you use regularly for learning. Prepare a short presentation to explain how it works. If possible, show the app or website to your classmates during your presentation.

LEARNING OBJECTIVES

Listening skill	Predict ideas from research
Pronunciation	Rising and falling intonation; vowel sounds /ɑ/ and /oʊ/
Speaking skill	Linking words to explain cause and effect
Speaking Task	Give a presentation about changes in the climate
On Campus	Manage your time

WEATHER AND CLIMATE

ACTIVATE YOUR KNOWLEDGE

Work with a partner. Look at the photo and answer the questions.

1 What kind of weather do you prefer when you are working, studying, or on vacation? Why?

2 How has the weather in your country changed? How does it affect people?

3 Have you ever experienced water shortages or floods? Do you do anything in your daily life to try and help with these problems?

WATCH AND LISTEN

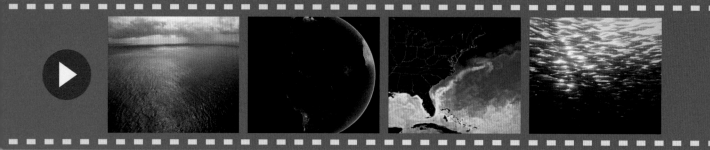

PREPARING TO WATCH

ACTIVATING YOUR KNOWLEDGE

1 Work with a partner and answer the questions.

1 How many oceans are there in the world? Can you name them?
2 How much of the Earth is covered by water?
3 Do you think oceans are important? Why or why not?

PREDICTING CONTENT USING VISUALS

2 Look at the diagram of Earth. Write a, b, c, d, or e in the statements. Compare your answers with a partner.

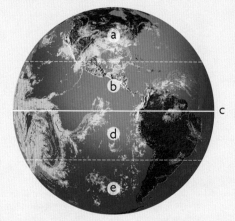

1 The weather is usually warm and sunny in _____ , _____ , and _____ .
2 The weather in _____ and _____ is usually cold in the winter.
3 Places near _____ are the hottest.
4 My country's weather is similar to the weather in _____ .

GLOSSARY

current (n) a movement of water or air

equator (n) the imaginary line around the Earth that divides it into equal north and south parts

gyre (n) a flow of water in a circle

heat (n) hot weather; extreme warmth

planet (n) a large, round object in space, such as Earth or Mars, that moves around the sun

WHILE WATCHING

3 ▶ Watch the video. Which parts of the diagram in Exercise 2 show ...

1 the equator?
2 the area north of the equator?
3 the area south of the equator?
4 the west coast of Chile in South America?

4 ▶ Write *T* (true) or *F* (false) next to the statements. Watch the video again and check your answers.

_____ 1 Water covers almost 50% of the Earth.
_____ 2 The water in the oceans moves around the planet.
_____ 3 South of the equator, currents move clockwise.
_____ 4 Ocean gyres are small circles of currents in the ocean.
_____ 5 These ocean currents keep water and heat in the same place.
_____ 6 Energy and heat from the equator changes our climate.
_____ 7 Ten percent of the fish we eat comes from a small part of the ocean near Chile.

5 Match the sentence halves. Compare your answers with a partner.

1 Water in the oceans moves because _____
2 Ocean gyres are important to climate because _____
3 There is warmer weather north of the equator because _____
4 South of the equator, ocean gyres are important because _____
5 It's a perfect place for fish to live because _____

a this water has lots of food in it.
b the Earth is spinning.
c warmer water from the equator moves north.
d they move water and heat.
e they move cooler water north along Chile in South America.

6 Work with a partner. The speaker in the video says that "without these ocean gyres, our world would be a very different place." What does the speaker mean?

DISCUSSION

7 Work with a partner or in small groups. Discuss the effects that heat has on ...

a the clothes we wear.
b the food we eat.
c the homes we live in.

LISTENING

LISTENING 1

PRONUNCIATION FOR LISTENING

Rising and falling intonation

Intonation describes how the tone of your voice goes up (rises) and goes down (falls). Intonation can help you understand someone's mood (e.g., happy, interested, excited, bored, sad, upset, etc.). Rising intonation can show interest or happiness. Falling intonation often shows boredom or sadness. Falling intonation can also show certainty.

really = The speaker is interested.

really = The speaker is not interested.

The meaning of a sentence can change depending on the intonation. Read the sentence aloud with a rising intonation and then a falling intonation. How does the meaning change?

I know.

PRISM Online Workbook

1 ▶ 4.1 Listen to the dialogues. Write *I* (interested) or *B* (bored) for Speaker B.

1 **A:** Did you know global warming is still increasing?
 B: Is it? _____

2 **A:** It's my birthday today.
 B: Really? Happy birthday! _____

3 **A:** The weather got really chilly, didn't it?
 B: I suppose so. _____

4 **A:** Thanks for inviting me to your party!
 B: You're welcome. It'll be nice to see you! _____

5 **A:** Dinner was great.
 B: Good. Glad you liked it. _____

2 Work with a partner. Read the dialogues aloud. Speaker B should change their intonation. Speaker A should guess whether Speaker B sounds interested or bored.

PREPARING TO LISTEN

3 Read the definitions. Write the correct form of the words in bold to complete the sentences.

> **angry** (adj) having a strong feeling against someone who has behaved badly, making you want to shout at them or hurt them; mad
> **cool** (adj) slightly cold; of a low temperature
> **dry** (adj) without water or liquid in, on, or around something
> **energy** (n) the power and ability to do something or be active
> **humid** (adj) having a lot of moisture in the air
> **prefer** (v) to choose or want one thing instead of another
> **upset** (adj) unhappy or worried because something unpleasant has happened

1 The weather was very hot and _____ today. People were sweating a lot because the air is very wet.
2 When it doesn't rain and the weather is very _____ , people worry that plants will die. There isn't enough water to help them grow.
3 I was _____ when it rained during my party at the park because the rain got all the food wet. No one was having fun outside.
4 I like _____ weather because it's nice and relaxing. Hot weather makes me feel very bad.
5 When the sun isn't out, some people feel sleepy and don't have _____ to get things done.
6 Some people get _____ in very hot weather. They become unfriendly and mean because the heat is too much to take.
7 Which type of weather do you _____ ? Do you like rainy weather or sunny weather?

4 You are going to listen to a discussion between two students who have been asked to prepare a survey about the weather and how it changes people's moods (how people feel). Work with a partner. How do you think different types of weather affect people's moods? Do you and your partner agree? Why or why not?

WHILE LISTENING

5 ▶ **4.2** Listen to part 1 of the discussion about weather and its effects on mood. Complete Sergio's notes on the idea map that organizes the effects of weather on people's moods.

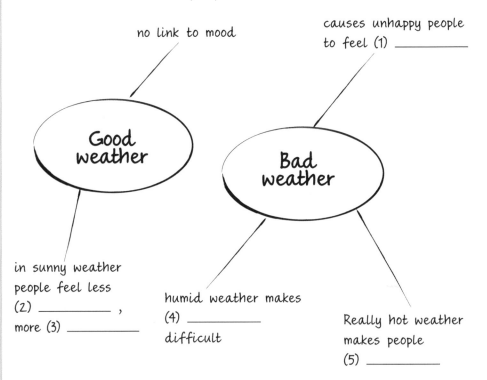

no link to mood

causes unhappy people to feel (1) _____

Good weather

Bad weather

in sunny weather people feel less (2) _____ , more (3) _____

humid weather makes (4) _____ difficult

Really hot weather makes people (5) _____

6 ▶ **4.2** Sergio and Murat have to choose the topic that they think is the most important. Match the topics to the reasons for choosing or not choosing them. Listen again to check your answers.

1 sunny weather (energy)
2 humid weather (work difficult)
3 bad weather (unhappy)
4 really hot weather (anger)

a wrong topic: not about feelings
b not sure if the facts are true
c final choice: Murat preferred it
d final choice: Murat didn't like it

7 ▶ **4.3** Listen to the results of the survey in part 2. Choose the correct results.

1 *Fourteen / Fifteen* people prefer sunny weather to rainy weather.
2 *Twelve / Thirteen* people said that they could get more done when there was sunshine.
3 Fourteen people said they have more energy when it is *light / dark*.
4 Sergio thinks the survey shows people have *more / less* energy when the weather is good.

DISCUSSION

8 Discuss the questions in pairs. Ask your partner follow-up questions.

   1 Can you think of an example when weather has changed your mood?

   2 Would it be easy for you to live in another country if the weather there was very different from the weather in your country?

⊙ LANGUAGE DEVELOPMENT

VERB COLLOCATIONS

1 Match the verbs to the nouns to make collocations. In some items, more than one answer is possible. Use a dictionary to help you.

PRISM Online Workbook

1	save	**a**	research
2	prevent	**b**	the rainforests
3	do	**c**	trees
4	cut down	**d**	global warming
5	cause	**e**	wildlife

2 Complete the sentences using the correct form of the verbs from Exercise 1.

   1 We should _____ forests by putting out campfires.

   2 We should _____ the plants in our garden if they get too big.

   3 We should _____ people from killing wildlife that is in danger of disappearing.

   4 Scientists need to _____ more research about the rainforests.

   5 Large amounts of carbon dioxide _____ global warming.

FUTURE FORMS

Decisions and plans

Use *will* to talk about decisions made at the time you are speaking.
Governments say they **will** stop the damage to forests.

Use *be going to* to talk about decisions made before you speak or a general plan that can change in the future.
Mr. Das **is going to** present information about the forests next week.

Use *the present progressive* (*be + -ing* form of a verb) to talk about fixed arrangements made for the future. It is difficult to change these arrangements.
During the next week, many people **are meeting** to talk about protecting the climate and saving the rainforests.

Predictions

Use *will* when you are guessing or are not certain about a future event. *Will* is often used with *probably*.
We need to plan now, or we **will probably** lose some species completely.

Use *be going to* to talk about a future event when there is evidence.
In fact, scientists believe 45 percent of the forest areas **are going to** change completely in the next 80 years.

PRISM Online Workbook

3 Use the future forms in parentheses and the underlined words to complete the dialogue.

Faisal: What are you doing tonight?

Anais: I have no idea. <u>I / probably / go home and do some reading</u>. (will)

(1) _____

How about you?

Faisal: Well, <u>I / visit Chile next month</u>. (present progressive)

(2) _____

So <u>I / make a hotel reservation</u>. (going to)

(3) _____

Anais: Wow! That sounds great. <u>I / come with you</u>! (will)

(4) _____

4 Write the correct future form of the verb in parentheses to complete the sentences. In some items, more than one answer is possible.

Decisions and plans

1 I just finished packing. I _____ (leave) tonight at six o'clock to catch the train.

2 I haven't finished my project on global warming because I don't have enough information. I decided that I _____ (do) some more research online.

3 "I _____ (go) to the garden center this weekend. Does anyone want to come?"
"OK, I _____ (come) with you."

4 Professor Lang _____ (talk) about global warming in his lecture tomorrow.

Predictions

5 You are carrying too many books! You _____ (drop) them.

6 The exam was really hard. I don't know if I _____ (pass).

5 Write an idea for each of the statements.

1 something I am going to do this weekend
  <u>I am planning to go hiking with my friends in the mountains.</u>

2 a place I will visit in the next year
  _____

3 something I am going to do in my studies or at work
  _____

4 an event I'm planning to go to
  _____

6 Work with a partner. Take turns telling each other the ideas you wrote.

PRONUNCIATION FOR LISTENING

SKILLS

Vowel sounds /ɑ/ and /oʊ/

Two easily confused vowel sounds are /ɑ/ and /oʊ/. You can hear the sound /ɑ/ in words like <u>o</u>n and j<u>o</u>b. You can hear the sound /oʊ/ in words like g<u>o</u> and c<u>o</u>ld.

PRISM Online Workbook

1 Say the words in Groups A and B aloud. Write the sound you hear in all of the words in each group (/oʊ/ or /ɑ/).

A _____ frog   stop   cost   want
B _____ global don't   known   won't

2 Work with a partner. Complete the sentences with the words from Exercise 1. Not every word will be used.

1 We _____ have a rainy season in my country. It's usually very dry.
2 Most people in my country _____ to stop climate change, but they don't know how.
3 I don't know if it is possible to _____ global warming or if it's too late.
4 People have _____ about global warming for a long time, but they haven't done much about it.
5 If we want to stop global warming, it will _____ a lot of money.

3 Work with a partner. Say the sentences in Exercise 2 aloud. Then decide if sentences 1–3 are true or false for you.

PREPARING TO LISTEN

PREDICTING CONTENT USING VISUALS

4 You are going to listen to a news report about global warming. Before you do, look at the photo of an animal mentioned in the report. Which type of animal do you think it shows? What kind of weather do you think an animal like this needs?

5 Read some information about the Western Ghats rainforest. Write the words in bold next to the definitions.

The Western Ghats is a tropical rainforest located in western India. The rainforest has a short dry period each year, but typically it gets a lot of rain. However, the type of weather in the forest is changing quickly, and global warming means that nowadays less rain falls. This is changing the forest itself; the environment is **becoming** damaged, and growth is stopping. The rainforest is home to **unusual** wildlife[1], which looks nothing like other wildlife in the world, and scientists are still **discovering** new species[2]. However, the damage to the rainforests means that some animals that can't be found anywhere else are **disappearing** because they are being killed by the changes in the climate. Many people **believe** that governments need to **save** the rainforests so that they will still be around in the future. They say it is important to **take care of** the forests and the animals so that climate change won't kill them. Researchers will have to look **carefully** for ways to fix global warming. They will need to really watch what is happening, take time to do research, and think about whether the solutions will help or not.

[1]**wildlife** (n) animals and birds living in the natural environment
[2]**species** (n) groups of plants or animals with similar characteristics

1 _____ (v) to think that something is true and correct
2 _____ (phr v) to care for or be responsible for someone or something
3 _____ (v) to stop existing in the world
4 _____ (adv) with great attention
5 _____ (v) to find something for the first time
6 _____ (v) to begin to be something
7 _____ (adj) different from what is common or expected
8 _____ (v) to bring something back to good condition; to keep something from harm

6 Summarize the information from Exercise 5 into three key points.

Key Points
1
2
3

7 Compare your key points with a partner. Did you choose the same points?

Predicting ideas from research

Before you listen to lectures, reports, or information about a topic, you often have time to prepare. It helps to read some information in advance. This can help you learn about the key topic and issues that people think are important. You can then predict the main ideas that you will hear.

8 Read the paragraph in Exercise 5 again. Check the things in the list that you think you will hear when you listen to the report.

1 city names ☐
2 information about the weather in the rainforest ☐
3 facts about wildlife ☐
4 the typical day of a scientist ☐
5 information about effects of global warming ☐

WHILE LISTENING

TAKING NOTES ON MAIN IDEAS

9 ▶ 4.4 Listen to the news report and take notes on the causes and effects. Use your notes to check your predictions from Exercise 8.

Cause	Effect
– Global warming ⟶	– Creates (1)_____ in rainforests in India global warming gets worse
– (2)_____ down trees ⟶	– (3)_____ forests more
– Worse global warming ⟶ – Increased temperature ⟶	– Stops normal forest growth, trees disappear
– Rainforests get less (4)_____ ⟶	– Changes how forests work
– Governments are not stopping damage to forests fast enough ⟶	– In next 80 years (5)_____ % of forest areas will change
– If we don't stop damage to forests ⟶	– Purple frog will (6)_____

10 ▶ 4.4 Listen again and choose the correct ending for the sentences.

1 Trees help prevent global warming because they ...
 a take in carbon dioxide.   b stop rainfall.

2 Scientists believe ...
 a 45 percent of the forest   b 80 percent of the forest
  will change.   will change.

3 The purple frog was discovered ...
 a in 2003.   b in 2009.

4 The problems are caused by ...
 a global warming.   b other animals.

5 The scientist believes ...
 a the frogs have disappeared.   b the frogs will disappear.

POST-LISTENING

11 Work with a partner. Look at the photos. What types of problems connected to climate change can you see?

North America

Brazil

China

12 Think about the plants and animals in the places in the photos and how climate change affects them. Make notes of your ideas.

13 Present your ideas to the class.

DISCUSSION

14 Use your notes from Listening 1 and Listening 2 to discuss the questions in pairs.

1 How do you think global warming affects people's mood over time?
2 How do you think the large changes in weather, climate, and environment might change how people act and feel?

SPEAKING

CRITICAL THINKING

At the end of this unit, you are going to do the Speaking Task below.

> Give a presentation about changes in the climate.

REMEMBER

1 Work with a partner. You are going to study climate change in the Arctic. What kind of weather is there in the Arctic? Make a list of how problems with the weather in the Arctic could affect people, animals, and the environment.

2 Work with a partner. Read the problems in the box for the Arctic. Did you and your partner have the same ideas?

THE ARCTIC

Temperatures rise.

Polar ice melts.

Sea levels rise.

Polar bears and other animals lose sea ice to hunt from.

Arctic animals begin to disappear.

People in the Arctic lose traditional food sources.

ANALYZE

3 Write the phrases from the box to complete the effects in the table. Use a dictionary to help you.

> sea levels rise   wildlife will begin to disappear   ~~ice will melt~~

causes of problem	effects of problem
The Arctic	
1 temperatures rise	a _ice melts_
2 ice melts	b _____
3 less sea ice for animals to hunt from	c _____

Evaluating effects

Using a cause-effect chain can help you to organize your thoughts before a speaking task. Use your cause-effect chain to evaluate the possible effects of events or decisions.

4 Work in small groups. Discuss the cause-effect chain for the Arctic.

EVALUATE ▲

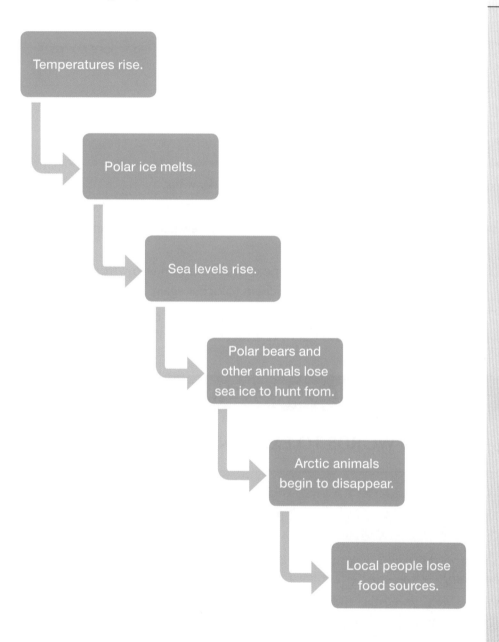

Temperatures rise.

Polar ice melts.

Sea levels rise.

Polar bears and other animals lose sea ice to hunt from.

Arctic animals begin to disappear.

Local people lose food sources.

CREATE

5 With your group, create your own cause-effect chain for Africa, low-level lands, or California. Use the ideas from the boxes below and your own ideas.

AFRICA

By 2050 up to 600 million people won't be able to get drinking water.

Drought will stop farmers from growing food.

Shortage of clean water will help diseases spread.

Some land areas will be under the ocean.

Some areas may lose up to 60% of animal species.

CALIFORNIA

Temperature rises.

Heat waves occur.

Less water is in the land.

Drought occurs.

Trees die.

Wildfires occur.

People lose homes and jobs.

LOW-LEVEL LANDS (MALDIVES, THE FLORIDA COASTLINE)

Ice on land melts around the world.

Sea levels rise.

Low-level land around the world floods.

Land areas go under water.

Some people lose their home or country.

People have to find new homes or countries to live in.

6 Can the cause-effect chain repeat? If so, draw an arrow from the box that could cause something in the chain to occur again.

 ANALYZE

7 Look at the words in the cause-effect chain you created. How exactly does one cause create the next effect?

PREPARATION FOR SPEAKING

LINKING WORDS TO EXPLAIN CAUSE AND EFFECT

 SKILLS

You can use words to let a listener know that what comes next will be an explanation of the cause of something. Examples of linking words for causes are *because*, *because of*, and *due to*.

You can also use linking words to show that what comes next is the effect of something. Examples of effect linking words are *so*, *therefore*, and *as a result*.

Word order is important to help the listener know if a cause or an effect will follow. The linking word should come right before the cause or effect.

1 Label the sentences in each pair *cause* or *effect*.

    1 **a** It is more difficult to work in high humidity. _____

        b Our concentration drops. _____

    2 **a** People feel more energy in sunny weather. _____

        b They can get a lot done if the sun is shining. _____

    3 **a** There isn't enough water for people to drink. _____

        b Some countries are very hot and don't get much rain. _____

2 ▶ 4.5 Listen to the sentences. Complete the sentences with the words you hear.

    1 It is more difficult to work in high humidity, _____ our concentration drops.

    2 People feel more energy in sunny weather. _____ , they can get a lot done if the sun is shining.

    3 Some countries are really hot and don't get much rain. _____ , there isn't enough water for people to drink.

3 Work with a partner. Think of an effect for each sentence. Use *so*, *therefore*, and *as a result* to show that an effect is coming next.

    1 The rainfall was too heavy.

        Therefore the village flooded.

    2 A new factory was built in the city.

        _____

    3 Nowadays, more people are interested in global warming.

        _____

    4 Rainforests are getting smaller.

        _____

    5 I lost my passport.

        _____

    6 Communication is much easier nowadays.

        _____

4 Choose sentences and effects from Exercise 3. Put the effect first, and explain the causes. Use *because of*, *because*, and *due to* to show that a cause is coming next.

    The village flooded (effect) due to the heavy rainfall (cause).

    1 _____

    2 _____

    3 _____

    4 _____

5 Compare your sentences with a partner.

6 Climate change is the effect of burning fossil fuels. Look at the pictures and try to understand the process.

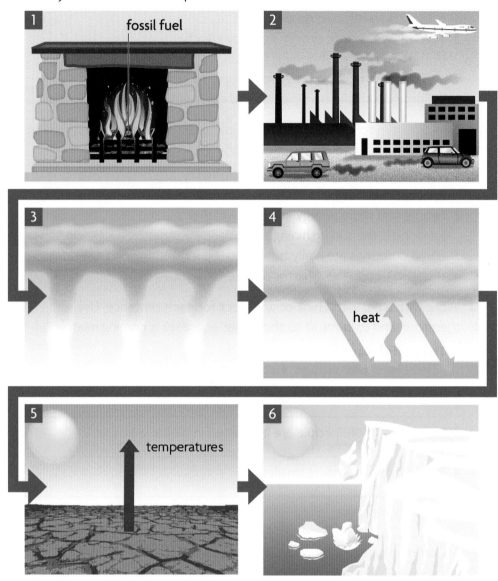

7 Work with a partner. Create a cause-effect chain to show how climate change can happen. Use the words in the box and a dictionary to help you.

burn	factory	gas(es)	heat	ice	melt	smoke	trap

8 Work with a partner. Describe the chain together. Use linking words from Exercises 3 and 4 to explain causes and effects.

SPEAKING TASK

> Give a presentation about changes in the climate.

PREPARE

1 Get back into the groups you worked with in Critical Thinking. Look back at your cause-effect chain and your group's discussion notes from Critical Thinking, Exercises 4–6. Add any new information you would like to include.

2 Add phrases to describe causes and effects to your notes. You can use language such as:

because   because of   due to   as a result   so   therefore

3 Refer to the Task Checklist below as you prepare your presentation.

TASK CHECKLIST	✔
Use collocations about weather and climate correctly.	
Use future forms correctly.	
Use sounds /ɑ/ and /oʊ/ correctly.	
Show interest when you respond.	
Use linking words like *because*, *because of*, and *due to* to show cause and *so*, *therefore*, and *as a result* to show effect.	

PRACTICE

4 Decide how your group will present. Practice your presentation so that you can change speakers smoothly.

PRESENT

5 Give a presentation about changes in the climate.

6 While listening to other groups, take notes on questions that you have. Then ask questions at the end of each presentation.

ON CAMPUS

MANAGING YOUR TIME

PREPARING TO LISTEN

1 You are going to listen to students talk about how to manage time in college. Before you listen, discuss the questions with a partner.

   1 Do college students have a lot of free time? Why or why not?

   2 How is a college schedule different from a high school schedule?

   3 What advice do you think the students will give?

WHILE LISTENING

2 ▶ **4.6** Read the statements. Then listen to the interview. Choose the best way to complete the statements.

1 When Grace first started college, she _____ .
   a missed her high school
   b had a lot of free time
   c studied very hard

2 When Roberto started college, he _____ .
   a missed his hometown
   b joined a lot of clubs
   c studied very hard

3 Grace and Roberto think that students should _____ .
   a enjoy their free time
   b join a lot of clubs
   c plan their time carefully

4 Grace likes to study _____ .
   a in the morning
   b in the afternoon
   c in the evening

3 ▶ **4.6** Listen again. Complete the students' advice.

1 Don't try to _____ ! Be realistic about _____ .

2 Use a _____ . You have to plan when _____ .

3 It's important to know _____ .

4 Take _____ ! Don't think you can _____ for six hours straight!

SKILLS

It is important to manage your time well when you are in college.

- Use a planner to keep track of classes, assignments and due dates.

- Don't take on too many extracurricular activities, such as clubs or sports.

- Know how, where, and when you study best.

- Take frequent short breaks from studying.

PRACTICE

4 Work with a partner. Look at this student's planner. Then add the following regular activities to the planner:

1 one hour each day for lunch and meeting with friends
2 one hour each day for dinner
3 three hours each week for exercising
4 one hour each week for an English study group
5 two hours each week for events, club meetings, etc., in the evening

	Today < >			Day Week Month 4 Days Agenda	☼ ▼
	Mon	**Tue**	**Wed**	**Thu**	**Fri**
8am		Bio 112		Bio 112	
9am		Bio Lab			
10am					
11am	Math 102		Math 102		Math 102
12pm		WORK		WORK	
1pm					
2pm	Chem 110		Chem 110		Chem 110
3pm					Chem Lab
4pm					
5pm					
6pm	English 106		English 106		English 106
7pm					
8pm					
9pm					

5 Work in small groups. Answer the questions.

1 Given this schedule, when could this student find time to study during the week?
2 What are the advantages and disadvantages of this schedule?
3 Do you like this schedule? Why or why not?

REAL-WORLD APPLICATION

6 Work with a partner. Compare your current schedules. Answer the questions.

1 What challenges do you have with your schedule?
2 How much time do you have for exercise and social events?
3 Would you change your schedule if you could? How?

LEARNING OBJECTIVES

Listening skills	Listen for bias; supporting opinions
Pronunciation	Make corrections
Speaking skills	Present a point; ask for and give clarification
Speaking Task	Have a discussion about money in sports
On Campus	Ask for information

SPORTS AND COMPETITION

ACTIVATE YOUR KNOWLEDGE

Work with a partner. Look at the photo and answer the questions.

1 Which sport and event can you see in the photo? Is this sport popular in your country?

2 Do you prefer to play individual or team sports? Why?

3 Do you like to win? Is it more important to win a competition or just to play for fun?

WATCH AND LISTEN

PREPARING TO WATCH

ACTIVATING YOUR KNOWLEDGE

1 Work with a partner and answer the questions.

  1 Can you name some popular board games?
  2 Why do people like to play games?
  3 How do people usually feel when they win or lose a game?

PREDICTING CONTENT

2 You are going to watch a video about a famous chess game. Decide which statements are true. Compare your answers with a partner.

  a You need to think a lot when you play chess.
  b Computers can play chess better than humans.
  c It doesn't take long to play a game of chess.

> **GLOSSARY**
>
> **escape** (v) to get away from a dangerous or bad situation
>
> **genius** (n) someone who is excellent at doing something; a very intelligent person
>
> **IBM** (n) the name of an American technology company
>
> **move** (n) in a game like chess, a change of the position of one of the pieces, or a person's turn to play
>
> **trick** (v) to make someone believe something that is not true

WHILE WATCHING

UNDERSTANDING MAIN IDEAS

3 ▶ Watch the video. Write *T* (true) or *F* (false) next to the statements. Correct the false statements.

  _____ 1 Humans began playing chess nearly 500 years ago.
  _____ 2 Garry Kasparov played a famous chess match against a child.
  _____ 3 An engineer moved the chess pieces.
  _____ 4 A computer can only calculate numbers to play chess.
  _____ 5 A genius like Kasparov can think about three moves a minute.

4 ▶ Watch again. Write the events in the correct column in the table.

a Garry Kasparov played the game very well.
b It seemed like the computer was thinking.
c The computer did not make a move for 15 minutes.
d In the end, the computer lost.
e The game took nearly four hours.
f Kasparov tried to escape the move, but he couldn't.

first game	second game

5 Work with a partner. Circle the correct answers.

UNDERSTANDING DETAILS

1 Where did humans begin playing chess?
  a India   b Russia
2 When did Garry Kasparov play a famous match?
  a in the 1980s   b in the 1990s
3 What is the computer's name?
  a Big Blue   b Deep Blue
4 How many moves can a computer think about in a second?
  a 20 million   b 200 million
5 What did Kasparov try to do in the second game?
  a to trick the computer   b to think of many moves
6 What did he do at the end of the second game?
  a he escaped   b he lost

6 The speaker in the video says that "to play chess well, you need many different skills." Work with a partner. Look at the skills in the box and decide which ones you need to be good at to play chess.

MAKING INFERENCES

> communication   computer programming   listening   math
> physical fitness   planning   teamwork   thinking

DISCUSSION

7 Work in small groups. Discuss the questions.

1 What other games can humans play against computers?
2 Is it better to play games against a human or a computer? Why?
3 Are computers getting smarter than humans? Give reasons.
4 How can computers help you learn to play and get better at games or sports?

LISTENING

LISTENING 1

PRONUNCIATION FOR LISTENING

Making corrections

When people speak, they sometimes make mistakes and correct themselves. If they correct themselves, they often emphasize the correct words. They do this with intonation and stress to make sure the people listening hear the change clearly.

OK, we're going to have a test tomorrow ... Oh, sorry, I mean <u>the day after tomorrow</u>.

PRISM Online Workbook

1 Underline the word that shows the correct information in the sentences.

1 The teacher's name isn't Mr. Rosso. It's Mr. Rosson.
2 I took a golf lesson, not a tennis lesson.
3 The game is at 6:00 tonight, not 6:30, so don't be late.
4 Yasmin doesn't take drama classes; she takes gymnastics classes.
5 The competition will be in Colombia, not in Brazil.

2 ▶ 5.1 Now listen to the sentences. Then answer the questions.

1 Which word does the speaker stress in each sentence?
2 Does the intonation go up or down?

3 Work with a partner. Take turns correcting the sentences by changing the underlined words to make them true or true for you. Then read the sentences aloud to each other. Be sure to use proper stress and intonation.

The most popular sport in my country, Canada, isn't soccer. It's ice hockey.

1 The most popular sport in my country is <u>basketball</u>.
2 My favorite sport is <u>bowling</u>.
3 The scoring system in soccer is based on points for <u>kicking the ball</u>.
4 We use a <u>football</u> to play tennis.
5 I study <u>sports science</u>.

PREPARING TO LISTEN

4 You are going to listen to a sports science student give a presentation about a project. Read the definitions. Write the correct form of the words in bold to complete the sentences.

> **champion** (n) someone who wins a competition
> **compete** (v) to do an activity with others and try to do it better than they do
> **hit** (v) to touch something quickly and forcefully with the hand or an object
> **intelligent** (adj) able to understand and learn well
> **kick** (v) to hit someone or something with the foot
> **strong** (adj) physically powerful

1 Which person needs to have really _____ arms, a baseball player or a golfer? They both want the ball to go a long way.
2 Chess players are often _____ people. They need to think a lot as they play and plan their moves.
3 Eduardo likes to _____ against others in sports like cycling. He is really fast and usually wins his races.
4 Roberto became the swimming _____ for our region. He beat all the other swimmers and got a medal as a prize.
5 In soccer, every player can _____ the ball with their feet, but can they use their hands sometimes?
6 In volleyball, can the players use their feet, or can they only _____ the ball with their hands?

5 Work with a partner. Check your answers in Exercise 4.

WHILE LISTENING

6 ▶ 5.2 Listen to a sports science student give a presentation about a project she did. Number the photos in the order she talks about them.

a   b   c   d

7 ▶ 5.2 Listen again. Complete the student's notes with important details.

Unusual Sports
- **Chess Boxing:** chess – (1)_____ players need to think carefully
  boxing – strong boxers have to (2)_____ each other
  do two activities – first (3)_____ , next (4)_____
  benefit – both mental and physical activity
- **Urban Golf:** play in the (5)_____ , not on golf course
  use golf clubs and (6)_____ balls
  advantages – don't need to go anywhere and don't need much
  (7)_____ to play
  disadvantage – might (8)_____ something if hit ball too hard
- **Sahara Marathon:** happens over (9)_____ days,
  longest-distance run in one day – 57 miles (92 kilometers)
  benefit: winner can say has won the (10)_____ race in world
- **Sepak Takraw:** type of volleyball, started in country of (11)_____
  players use different balls and use (12)_____ , knees, chest,
  or (13)_____
  popular in Southeast Asia, Thailand, Indonesia
  benefit – gets children to play sports because played in (14)_____
  in many countries

8 ▶ 5.3 Listen to the excerpts from Listening 1. Cross out the mistake that Yasmin makes in each sentence below. Then write the correct word.

1 In chess boxing, they begin with boxing and then switch.

2 For urban golf, you use golf clubs and a golf ball to play.

3 The Sahara Marathon happens over a week in Morocco.

4 Sepak Takraw began in Indonesia and is very popular.

POST-LISTENING

9 Use the phrases that Yasmin used to correct her mistakes and complete the sentences. Refer to Exercise 8 to help you. Listen again to check answers.

> no, not   or rather   sorry, I mean   well, actually

1 They start with boxing – _____ chess.
2 You get clubs and a golf ball – _____ , it is a soft tennis ball instead of a hard golf ball.
3 This race is held every year over a week – _____ over six days.
4 The sport began in Indonesia and it – _____ Indonesia – it began in Malaysia.

10 Choose a popular sport. Write a sentence about the sport, but include a factual mistake in it.

_____

11 Work with a partner. Take turns reading your sentence from Exercise 10 aloud. Then correct it using the phrases from Exercise 9.

In soccer you need ten players. Well, actually, you need 11 players, 10 to play and a goalie.

DISCUSSION

12 Work in small groups. Use your notes to help you as you discuss with your group. Talk about which of the sports from the presentation you would like to watch or try. Why are you interested in that sport? Do you want to try it or just watch it? Why? Ask follow-up questions.

CONDITIONALS

> **LANGUAGE**
>
> ### Factual and future real conditionals
>
> Use a *factual conditional* to talk about facts, habits, and routine things that happen under certain conditions. Use the simple present in both the *if* clause and the result clause. You can also use modals in the result clause.
>
> | *if clause* | *result clause* |
> |---|---|
>
> If you **play** urban golf, you **don't need** to go anywhere special.
>
> | *if clause* | *result clause* |
> |---|---|
>
> If you **hit** the ball too hard, you **might break** something.
>
> Use a *future real conditional* to talk about things that will happen under certain conditions in the future. Use the simple present in the *if* clause and a future form in the result clause. You can also use modals in the result clause.
>
> If company sponsors **don't support** the Olympics, the Olympics **will** have to charge more for tickets.
>
> If companies **sponsor** lots of athletes, more people **could participate** in competitions.

PRISM Online Workbook

1 Complete each sentence with an appropriate result clause. Put the words in the correct order using the correct verb form.

Use factual conditionals

1 (and / intelligent / need / he or she / strong / to be)
If a person plays chess boxing, _____
_____ .

2 (of the hardest race / they can / the champion / say they are / in the world)
If a person wins the Sahara Marathon, _____
_____ .

3 (health / might / he or she / bad / have)
If a person doesn't exercise, _____
_____ .

4 (catch / you / a ball near your seat / might)
If you go to a U.S. baseball game, _____
_____ .

5 (you can / types / many / watch / of sports)

If you go to the Olympics, _____

_____ .

Use future real conditionals

6 (the / national champions / be / they)

If my team wins the game on Saturday, _____

_____ .

7 (you / golf clubs / need to buy)

If you decide to try urban golf, _____

_____ .

8 (have / more / you / strength)

If you start to lift weights, _____

_____ .

9 (she / be / successful)

If your friend tries out for the volleyball team, _____

_____ .

10 (cancel / they / it)

If it rains hard during the game tomorrow, _____

_____ .

2 Work with a partner. Check your answers from Exercise 1. Discuss any answers that are different.

3 Write four conditional sentences (factual or future) about sports or activities that you do.

If I ride my bicycle to work every day, I will ride 400 miles by the end of the month.

1 If I play my favorite sport, I _____

_____ .

2 If I have free time on the weekend, I _____

_____ .

3 If I get a chance to learn a new sport next summer, I _____

_____ .

4 If my friend wants to do something unusual this weekend, I _____

_____ .

4 Work with a partner. Take turns sharing your sentences from Exercise 3. Ask follow-up questions.

ADVERBS OF DEGREE

Adverbs of degree can make other adverbs or adjectives stronger or weaker.

weaker   stronger

somewhat   really   very   extremely

The runner was **somewhat** fast. (weakens the adjective)
The tickets for the game were **really** expensive, so I couldn't go. (strengthens the adjective)

Do not use *somewhat* in negative sentences.
The runner wasn't ~~somewhat~~ fast. The runner wasn't **really** fast.

Really is more common in speaking than *extremely* and *very*.

PRISM Online Workbook

5 Match the adverb of degree to the definition.

1 extremely   a very (informal)
2 really   b to a great degree
3 somewhat   c much more than usual
4 very   d slightly

6 Write an adverb of degree to complete the sentences. In some items, more than one answer is possible. Then decide if the adverb of degree makes the adjective or adverb stronger (S) or weaker (W).

1 Soccer is ___very___ popular as a sport all around the world. __S__
2 I don't go to see professional games often because they are _____ expensive. _____
3 However, I do go to see local games because they are _____ cheap. _____
4 Sophia is _____ competitive. In fact, this weekend she will run in two races. _____
5 Mehmet's _____ tired because he just ran five miles. _____
6 The coach said the team would arrive at six o'clock, but they arrived at five o'clock. I think they were _____ early. _____

7 Work with a partner. Share your answers.

8 Think of an idea for each of the statements.

1 Something you can somewhat do.
2 Something that you are really good at.
3 Something that is extremely interesting to you.

9 Work with a partner. Take turns telling each other your ideas.

PREPARING TO LISTEN

UNDERSTANDING
KEY VOCABULARY

PRISM Online Workbook

1 You are going to listen to a discussion about money in sports. Read the sentences. Write the words in bold next to the definitions.

1 Big tennis **competitions** like the U.S. Open, the French Open, and Wimbledon are held every year.

2 **Fans** from around the world come to watch their favorite tennis players compete against each other.

3 The **cost** of putting together and organizing these tennis matches is very high. Organizers have to pay a lot of money.

4 Organizers sometimes **charge** people a lot of money for tickets to a big sporting event.

5 Most athletes are not paid a **salary**, which people get when they have a full-time job.

6 Sometimes a company or a government will pay athletes money to **support** them and make sure they have enough money to train.

7 When a soccer team **scores** the most points in a match, they win.

8 The winner of the tennis match will get a big **prize** of $600,000 and a medal.

a _____ (n) something valuable that is given to someone who wins a game or has done good work

b _____ (v) to ask someone to pay for something, especially for an activity or a service

c _____ (v) to get points in a game or on a test

d _____ (n) the amount of money that you need to buy or do something

e _____ (n) the amount of money that you get from your job, usually every two weeks or every month

f _____ (n) someone who likes a famous person, sport, type of music, etc.

g _____ (v) to take care of someone by paying for his or her food, clothes, etc.

h _____ (n) an organized event in which people try to win by being the best, the fastest, etc.

WHILE LISTENING

Listening for bias

Before listening, think about who is talking and why. Sometimes people are *biased*. They will have a reason to agree or disagree with something. For example, a business that is trying to get advertising might say it is OK to pay to have their name on a stadium. But a sports fan might want to have a stadium named after a famous athlete. So if you think about people and what they care about, this can give you information about what they might think before they speak. You can then listen for words that help you understand their opinions.

PRISM Online Workbook

2 Andre and Chen will discuss if companies should pay athletes to train. Read the descriptions. Then write *Andre* or *Chen* next to the opinions.

Chen: a longtime sports fan   **Andre:** a college soccer player

_____ 1 Obviously, Olympic soccer teams should be able to take money from companies for support.

_____ 2 Actually, seeing advertisements everywhere at the Olympics is really annoying.

LISTENING FOR BIAS

3 ▶ 5.4 Listen to the discussion. Check your predictions in Exercise 2.

1 What bias does Chen, the fan, have?
2 What bias does Andre, the athlete, have?

TAKING NOTES ON OPINION

4 ▶ 5.4 Listen again and complete the student's notes showing reasons for and against companies paying large amounts of money to athletes.

<u>Athletes should be able to take money from companies to help with their training.</u>

agree	disagree
• <u>Reason:</u> without the (1)_____ , athletes have no job	• <u>Reason:</u> all athletes are interested in is making huge (7)_____ of money
<u>Support:</u> athletes can't live, work, and pay for training; cost of training is really high	<u>Support:</u> more marketing than ever
• <u>Reason:</u> athletes need good training	• <u>Reason:</u> athletes are like (8)_____
<u>Support:</u> no medals, lose chance to (2)_____ ; only (3)_____ % of Olympic athletes get money from companies	<u>Support:</u> get paid to wear companies' names on clothing; (9)_____ contracts
• <u>Reason:</u> poorer countries can't pay the costs for (4)_____	• <u>Reason:</u> athletes should represent their (10)_____
<u>Support:</u> more people can (5)_____	<u>Support:</u> there would be less pressure to get money from a company
• <u>Reason:</u> good for everyone – players, (6)_____ , fans	• <u>Reason:</u> all the money takes away from Olympics
<u>Support:</u> everyone gets money or cheaper costs	<u>Support:</u> see (11)_____ everywhere

POST-LISTENING

SKILLS

Supporting opinions

When speakers give an opinion, they need to support it with information and facts. Support can come from places like the news, books, the Internet, magazines, or personal experiences.

5 Work with a partner. Read the sentences from the listening. Is the speaker giving an opinion or giving information to support an opinion? Write *S* for support or *O* for only opinion.

1 It seems like the athletes are more interested in making money than in representing their countries. _____

2 Without all the help from companies, he might not have enough money to play tennis as his "job." _____

3 And actually, only about 5 percent of Olympic athletes get money from big companies to be in ads. _____

4 I read that in the U.K., the government pays the country's Olympic athletes to train, so there is less pressure there to get money from a company. _____

DISCUSSION

6 Work with a partner. Use your notes from Listening 1 and Listening 2 to discuss the questions.

SYNTHESIZING

1 Are sports important for countries and people in general? Why?

2 What do fans and athletes get from sports?

3 The Olympic Games only allows some sports to participate. Should unusual sports be included in the Olympics? Why or why not?

tennis player
Novak Djokovic

SPEAKING

At the end of this unit, you are going to do the Speaking Task below.

> Have a discussion about money in sports. Discuss arguments for and against athletes being paid extremely large amounts of money.

REMEMBER

1 Work with a partner. Answer the questions.

1 What are some reasons for an athlete to participate in a big sports competition like the Olympics or the World Cup?

_____

_____

_____

2 Why do companies want to support athletes at big competitions?

_____

_____

_____

3 What are two reasons why some fans don't like the idea of companies supporting athletes?

_____

_____

_____

APPLY

2 Work with a partner. Decide which sentences give a reason for companies to support athletes and which give a reason against it. Write *for* or *against*.

1 Sport fans like to see ads with athletes in them. _____
2 Companies are taking advantage of athletes that need money for training. _____
3 Companies can advertise to a lot of fans all at once. _____
4 Athletes are able to use their talents to make money, even if they don't win competitions. _____
5 Fans are seeing more and more ads during sporting events. _____
6 Athletes without companies' support are not able to train as much or succeed. _____

Using a persuasion map

A persuasion map helps you organize your ideas about a point. It gives you a place to write reasons *for* a point (you agree with an idea) or *against* a point (you disagree with it). It also helps you organize support for your reasons (evidence for why your opinion is correct). Using a persuasion map can help you organize your ideas when you want to get others to agree with your point of view.

3 Work in a group of three or four. Read your role card on page 190 (Student A, Student B, Student C, Student D) to prepare for the Speaking Task at the end of this unit.

4 After reading your role card, decide if you (as the person in the role) are *for* or *against* the argument. Choose an option to complete the sentence in the box. Think about reasons why your role might be for or against. Write three reasons in the persuasion map.

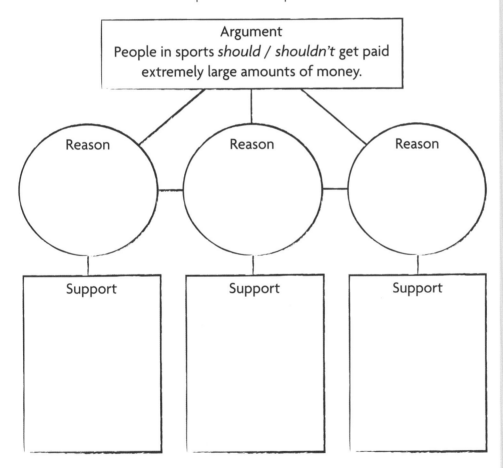

Argument
People in sports *should / shouldn't* get paid
extremely large amounts of money.

Reason   Reason   Reason

Support   Support   Support

5 Now add one example or fact to support each reason. You can use information from Listening 2 or your own ideas. You will use this persuasion map for the Speaking Task at the end of this unit.

PRESENTING POINTS AND CLARIFYING STATEMENTS

> **SKILLS**
>
> **Presenting a point**
>
> When you discuss a topic with others, you can use signal words to help you make that point strongly.
>
> *Of course*, *obviously*, *actually*, and *definitely* all signal to the listener that what comes next is going to be a point that you wish to emphasize.

PRISM Online Workbook

1 ▶ 5.5 Listen to the sentences from Listening 2. Use the words from the box to complete the sentences.

| actually   definitely   obviously   of course |

1 I think there is _____ more marketing and business in sports than ever before.

2 And _____ , only about 5 percent of Olympic athletes get money from big companies to be in ads.

3 Well, _____ poorer countries can't usually pay the costs for training athletes.

4 And _____ , the countries with lots of money can train their athletes really well.

2 Write sentences to give reasons and support either for or against the points you made in Exercises 4 and 5 in Critical Thinking. Use a word from the box above to emphasize your point in each sentence.

Sports fans actually like to see ads with athletes in them.

a _____

b _____

c _____

d _____

3 Work with a partner who chose the same point of view as you in Exercise 2. Share your sentences. Discuss your argument, reasons, and support. Do you have similar ideas?

Asking for and giving clarification

Sometimes in a persuasive discussion, it isn't always clear what point someone is making.

If you don't understand what someone has said, you can use expressions like:

Sorry, I didn't follow what you said.

I'm afraid I didn't get that.

What do you mean by ... ?

I'm sorry, I don't understand.

If you want someone to explain more, you can use expressions like:

Could you give an example?

Can you go into more detail?

Can you explain what you mean?

When someone asks you to clarify your point or idea, you can use these expressions:

Sorry, let me explain ...

To put it differently ...

In other words ...

Sure, for example ...

PRISM Online Workbook

4 Discuss the questions in pairs. Try to ask for and give clarification as you talk about your ideas.

1 The photo shows a Sepak Takraw competitor. One rule of Sepak Takraw is that the Tekong (the person who serves the ball) can't jump off the ground when she or he serves the ball. Another rule is that you cannot shout at the other team. Do you think that these are good rules? Why?

2 Why do you think it's important to have rules in sports? Give support for your reasons.

5 An interviewer (*I*) is speaking to a Sepak Takraw competitor (*C*). Put the sentences in each part of the interview in the correct order, from 1–6.

Part 1

I: *What do you mean by Tekong?* _____

C: Yes, I thought we played well. We made a few silly mistakes, though. _____

C: That's the player who serves the ball during the match ... _____

I: Which mistakes did you make? *Can you go into some more detail?* _____

C: Yeah, sure. I thought that the ball went outside the court too much. Also, our Tekong jumped off the ground once or twice. _____

I: Did you enjoy the game? __1__

Part 2

C: Sure. One example is the excitement in the game from the players' amazing kicks ... _____

C: Definitely! I agree that it should be included. It's already in the Asian Games. _____

I: Can you give some examples of why people want to see this sport in the Olympics? _____

I: But even though it is in the Asian games, can you explain more of why you support it? _____

C: Well, obviously, as a player I support it. But actually, even people who are not players want to see it in the Olympics. _____

I: I hear that people are trying to get Sepak Takraw included in the Olympics. Do you agree? _____

6 Work with a partner. Look at the questions in italics from Exercise 5, Part 1. What is another way to ask each of these questions of clarification?

7 Look at the interview from Exercise 5, Part 2. Underline the phrases that show ways of asking a person to explain more. Circle the phrases that show that the person is emphasizing a point.

8 Work with a partner. Check your answers for Exercise 7.

9 Look at the phrases. Write *DU* (I don't understand) and *EM* (I want you to explain more).

1 Sorry, I didn't follow what you said. _____
2 Can you explain what you mean? _____
3 I'm afraid I didn't get that. _____
4 I'm sorry, but I don't understand. _____
5 Would you mind giving me some examples? _____

10 Work in a group of three. Follow the steps.

1 Choose a popular sport or activity.
2 Think of reasons why people would or wouldn't want to take part in the competition.
3 Think of support (facts or examples) for each reason you come up with.

11 Work with someone from another group. Follow the steps.

1 Take turns explaining your ideas from Exercise 10 to each other. Try to use phrases to emphasize your points.

2 Ask each other for more information if you don't understand. Ask for support for reasons, if none are given.

SPEAKING TASK

Have a discussion about money in sports. Discuss reasons for and against athletes being paid extremely large amounts of money.

PRISM Online Workbook

PREPARE

1 Get back into your groups from Critical Thinking. Read your role cards again on page 190 (Student A, Student B, Student C, Student D).

2 Look back at your persuasion map from Exercises 4 and 5 in Critical Thinking. Add any new information.

3 Refer to the Task Checklist below as you prepare your panel discussion.

TASK CHECKLIST	✔
Use conditional forms correctly.	
Use key vocabulary to talk about sports.	
Ask for and give clarification using the correct language.	
Use signal words to clearly present your points.	
Give reasons and support (e.g., facts and examples) when presenting a point.	

DISCUSS

4 Have the panel discussion in your roles. Take turns stating your ideas before a general discussion. Student A should start. Remember to talk about your reasons *for* or *against* and give support for those reasons. Ask for clarification if you need to.

ASKING FOR INFORMATION

PREPARING TO LISTEN

1 You are going to hear a professor announce a test. Work with a partner. What kinds of questions do you think the students will ask?

WHILE LISTENING

2 ▶ 5.6 Listen to the excerpt. Did the students ask the questions that you expected?

3 ▶ 5.6 Listen again and circle the correct answer.

1 The test will take place on *Friday / Monday*.
2 Students will complete the test *online / on paper*.
3 Students *may / may not* use dictionaries.
4 The test will take about *one hour / two hours*.
5 There are *five / seven* questions on the test.
6 The students need to read *two chapters / three chapters* in the textbook.
7 The test counts for *30% / 40%* of the final grade.

4 ▶ 5.6 Listen again. Complete the questions.

1 _____ use our laptops?
2 _____ to use dictionaries?
3 _____ will it take?
4 _____ of test is it?
5 _____ prepare?
6 _____ of our grade is it?

SKILLS

Ask questions to check that you understand information from professors and administrators.

Can I … ?
Is it possible / OK to … ?
Where / When / How long is … ?
What / How / Who / Where should I … ?

PRACTICE

5 Read the questions. Then match them to the answers.

1 Can I turn in my paper on Monday? _____
2 Is it OK to email you if I have a question? _____
3 Is it possible to keep that book out until tomorrow? _____
4 Which classes do I have to take? _____
5 When is the deadline to add a class? _____
6 How can I apply for a job on campus? _____
7 What materials do I need for the class? _____

a I'm sorry, but someone else has reserved it.
b It's not due until Tuesday, but you can turn it in early if you like.
c Just a notebook and a calculator.
d Let me see ... I think you have to take calculus, and probably a writing class.
e There's an online form to fill out.
f Tomorrow is the last day to add.
g Yes. But give me 24 hours to reply.

6 Read the questions and answers again. Which questions would you ask each of the people below? (Some questions can apply to several people.)

1 a librarian _____
2 an administrator or office clerk _____
3 an advisor _____
4 a teacher or professor _____

REAL-WORLD APPLICATION

7 Work with a partner. Think of three questions that you might ask at each of these places on campus.

library

cafeteria

gym

8 Role-play a conversation between a student and an administrator or teacher. Include some of your questions from Exercise 7 in the conversation.

LEARNING OBJECTIVES

Listening skill	Listen for numbers
Pronunciation	Pronounce numbers
Speaking skill	Give advice
Speaking Task	Give advice to a failing business
On Campus	Work in groups

ACTIVATE YOUR KNOWLEDGE

Work with a partner. Look at the photo and answer the questions.

1 What type of job do you think the person in the photo is doing?
2 Could you work in an office like this?
3 What kind of job would you do if money wasn't important?
4 What are the advantages and disadvantages of working?

PREPARING TO WATCH

ACTIVATING YOUR KNOWLEDGE

1 Work with a partner and answer the questions.

1 Can you name some famous coffee companies?
2 Why do people like to go to coffee shops?
3 What are some things that coffee shops usually sell?

PREDICTING CONTENT

2 You are going to watch a video about the coffee business. Work with a partner. Discuss the statements. Do you agree or disagree?

1 Starbucks is the most popular coffee shop in the world.
2 People spend more money on coffee than on food in coffee shops.
3 People around the world prefer coffee from South America.

GLOSSARY

chain (n) a number of similar stores, restaurants, etc. owned by the same company

model (n) a type of machine, car, or business

customer (n) a person or organization that buys things or services from a store or business

headquarters (n) the main office of a company or organization

consultant (n) an expert in a particular subject who gives advice and information to businesses

---

WHILE WATCHING

3 ▶ Watch the video. Write the letter of the correct answer in the blank.

1 _____ coffee shops are growing quickly in Great Britain.
   a Starbucks   **b** Caffè Nero

2 Caffè Nero opened its first American store in _____ .
   a New York   **b** Boston

3 Gerry Ford _____ this coffee chain.
   a started   **b** bought

4 Ford wants his customers to spend more money on _____ in his coffee shops.
   a food   **b** coffee

5 Ford's coffee chain uses an _____ model.
   a American   **b** Italian

4 ▶ Watch again. Work with a partner and circle the correct answer.

1 Starbucks and *Caffè Nero / Costa Coffee* are two of the biggest coffee chains in the world.

2 Caffè Nero is always busy for *lunch / dinner*.

3 Caffè Nero is *a British / an Italian* company.

4 Thirty percent of its sales are in *food / drinks*.

5 A food consultant helps the company at its *coffee shops / headquarters*.

6 It is important to the company to sell *cheap / quality* food and coffee.

5 Work with a partner. Choose the best summary for the main idea of the video.

a Gerry Ford tries to sell sandwiches and cookies that people will like.
b Gerry Ford's company has a successful business model.
c Gerry Ford's company doesn't try to copy other big coffee chains.

6 Work with a partner. Why do you think it is important to give American customers Americanized food? Share your answers with another partner.

DISCUSSION

7 Discuss the questions with a partner or in small groups.

1 What are the most popular coffee chains in your city or country?
2 What do coffee chains like Starbucks have in common?
3 Besides food and coffee, what are some other important things for coffee shop customers?

8 Imagine that you are working for Gerry Ford. What are some new ideas to get customers to spend more money in his coffee shops? Share your ideas with the class.

LISTENING

LISTENING 1

PREPARING TO LISTEN

1 Read the definitions. Write the correct form of the words in bold to complete the sentences.

> **break** (n) a stop in an activity for a short time
> **colleague** (n) someone who works with you
> **earn** (v) to get money from doing work
> **profit** (n) money that you make from selling goods or services for more than they cost to make or provide
> **project** (n) a piece of work that is for a particular purpose or a detailed study of a topic
> **spend time** (v phr) to use time to do something
> **waste time** (v phr) to use time badly

1 I don't _____ much money. My job doesn't pay very much, and it is only part-time.

2 I was talking with some coworkers when another _____ came by and reminded us of a meeting with the boss.

3 Isabel _____ planning her tasks at the beginning of every workday because she wants to use her time well.

4 Looking at silly cat videos on the Internet at work _____ that your company is paying you for.

5 Taryn's fashion company makes a big _____ . She doesn't pay much money for the materials or for the work to make the clothes, and she sells them for a higher price.

6 In college I had to study and do a lot of library research on a _____ for my engineering course.

7 At 12:00 p.m., all the workers took a _____ for lunch.

PRONUNCIATION FOR LISTENING

Pronouncing numbers

The way a number is pronounced may be different if the number is used in math, science, or banking.

Fractions: You may hear *a* or *one* in front of a fraction:

½ is *a half* or *one half*; ⅓ is *a third* or *one third*, etc.

Decimals: You may hear the word *point* in decimals. For example:

0.27 is *zero point twenty-seven* or *zero point two seven*.

Percentages: % is pronounced *percent* and is read directly after the number. For example:

27% is *twenty-seven percent*.

2 You are going to listen to a business student speak about a project that includes different numbers. Work with a partner. Say the numbers aloud.

1 48%
2 ½
3 ⅕
4 31.5

5 103
6 1,540
7 6,001

3 6.1 Listen to the numbers and repeat.

WHILE LISTENING

Listening for numbers

Numbers are difficult to hear if they are said quickly or if they are very long. You need to understand the numbers but also any words related to them, e.g., *percent* and *point*. Practice listening to and writing numbers as much as you can.

4 ▶ 6.2 Listen to a conversation between a university professor and a student about her project. Take notes in Alika's outline of her research. Listen for numbers and words related to numbers.

How people waste time at work

Internet and Online use: almost (1)_____ of all workers wasted time surfing Internet or writing personal (2)_____

(3)_____ % spent time talking to colleagues

(4)_____ % took longer coffee and lunch breaks

5% texting friends

Why people waste time at work

½ not happy with (5)_____

⅓ thought they didn't (6)_____ a good enough salary

not enough $ for vacations and nice (7)_____

(8)_____ % have to work too many hours

Effects on companies

Workers don't work hard; productivity goes down

So company makes less money than it wanted to

Company can't pay workers higher (9)_____

5 ▶ 6.2 Listen again. Write *T* (true) or *F* (false) next to the statements. Then correct the false statements.

_____ 1 Alika has finished her research project.

_____

_____ 2 She read a lot of reports.

_____

_____ 3 Alika looked at why people like or dislike their jobs.

_____

_____ 4 People waste time at work by surfing the Internet, talking to other people, and taking long breaks.

_____

_____ 5 Half of the workers waste time because they don't earn enough money.

_____

6 ▶ 6.2 Listen again and look at the bar graphs. Then write sentences showing how people wasted time at work (1–4) and the reasons for wasting time (5–6). Make sure your sentences match the data in the graphs.

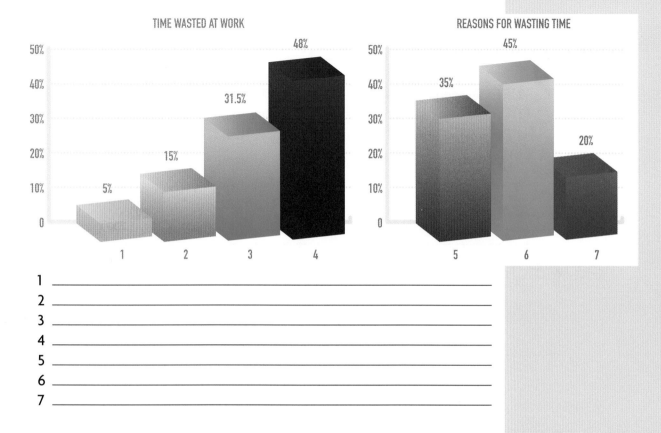

1 _____
2 _____
3 _____
4 _____
5 _____
6 _____
7 _____

DISCUSSION

7 Work with a partner. Choose two ideas from the list that will stop people from wasting time at work. Why do you think these ideas will work?

  1 Make sure everyone has a regular break.
  2 Pay a very high salary.
  3 Shout at people who waste time.
  4 Give extra pay to people who work quickly.

8 Do you agree or disagree with these sentences? Why?

  1 Earning a lot of money is more important than having a fun job.
  2 The most exciting work is having your own business.
  3 Younger people do not have enough experience to be good managers.
  4 Older people with families don't work as hard as young, single people.
  5 People who work the longest hours do the most work.
  6 The best time to begin working is after you graduate from college.

COMPARATIVES AND SUPERLATIVES

LANGUAGE

Comparing quantities

1 People wasted **the most** time on the Internet.
2 People spent **the least** time texting friends.
3 People spent **less** time texting than talking to people.
4 People spent **more** time talking to people than taking long breaks.

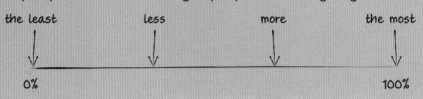

PRISM Online Workbook

1 Use the information in the table to complete the sentences.

time spent working at a desk	60%
time spent taking breaks	25%
time spent in meetings	10%
time spent on the phone	5%

1 People spent **the least** amount of time _____ .
2 People spent **less** time _____ than taking breaks.
3 People spent **the most** time _____ .
4 People spent **more** time _____ than in meetings.

2 Write four sentences using the words in bold in Exercise 1 and the information in the table below.

work-related reasons for not using time well	% of people
1 helping someone else with their work	54%
2 waiting for someone to finish her or his part of a project	42%
3 going to meetings	30%
4 filling out paperwork and forms	18%

1 _____
2 _____
3 _____
4 _____

LANGUAGE

Comparatives (comparing two things)

If an adjective is one syllable, add -er to make a comparative.
young / old → **younger / older**

If there are two or more syllables, use the words *more* or *less* before the adjective and the word *than* after the adjective.
important → **more important than / less important than**

You can show two things are the same with *as* + adjective + *as*.
My salary is **as much as** your salary.

Superlatives (comparing one thing to a group)

If an adjective is one syllable, use the word *the* and add -est to the end of the adjective.
big → **the biggest**

If there are two or more syllables, use the word *the* and *most* or *least* before the adjective.
experienced → **the most experienced / the least experienced**

Some adjectives are irregular. Memorize their comparative and superlative forms.
good → **better** → **the best**   bad → **worse** → **the worst**

3 Complete the sentences. Change the word in parentheses to a comparative or superlative. Add words like *than*, *as*, or *the* to make the correct phrase.

Does Sally work ___harder than___ (hard) you?

1 Is money _____ (important) having an interesting job?
2 Is a job working inside as _____ (good) a job working outside?
3 Do you think men are _____ (bad) women at organizing things?
4 Which of your friends types _____ (fast) you?
5 Who has _____ (neat) handwriting in your family?
6 Which job do you think is _____ (exciting) in the world?

4 Choose three classmates and ask them the questions in Exercise 3.

PHRASAL VERBS

Phrasal verbs can be used with objects. Sometimes the object goes **either** between the verb and the particle **or** after the verb and the particle.

verb + object + particle
You **wrote** a lot of information **down**.
I **found** a lot of information **out**.

verb + particle + object
I **wrote down** a lot of information.
I **found out** a lot of information.

Sometimes the object can **only** go after the verb and the particle. When this happens, the phrasal verb is *inseparable*.

verb + particle + object (inseparable)
I **ran out of time**.
I **took part in the discussion** on productivity.
I **looked at how people spend time** at work.

Some phrasal verbs don't take an object. When this happens, the phrasal verb is *intransitive*.
A third of people had just enough money to **get by**.

PRISM Online Workbook

5 Underline the phrasal verbs. Then label them as *v + p + o* (*inseparable*), *v + p + o*, *v + o + p*, or *intransitive*.

1 You <u>wrote</u> a lot of information <u>down</u>. _____v + o + p_____

2 I haven't finished yet – I ran out of time. _____

3 I wrote down notes from my research. _____

4 I took part in the discussions with my colleagues.

_____

5 I found out a lot of information about the way people work.

_____

6 I found a lot of interesting information out from my study group.

_____

7 ... I looked at how people spend time at work. _____

8 They had just enough money to get by each month.

_____

6 Write the base form of the phrasal verbs from Exercise 5 next to the definitions. Use a dictionary to check your answers.

verb	definition
1 _____	to use all of something
2 _____	to read or think about something carefully
3 _____	to get information for the first time
4 _____	to be able to live by having just enough of what you need, usually with difficulty
5 _____	to make or write a note
6 _____	to do an activity with other people

7 Match the sentence halves. Use the phrasal verbs in bold to help you.

1 Would you like to **take** _____
2 If you have to **find** _____
3 Do you **write** _____
4 Have you ever **run out** _____
5 Experts need to **look** _____

a **up** a new hobby? What would you do?
b **at** why people are getting sick from the water.
c **out** new information, where do you look?
d **of** money while you were out? How did you **get by**?
e **down** phone numbers or put them right into your phone?

8 Work with a partner. Ask and answer the questions in Exercise 7.

PREPARING TO LISTEN

1 Read the definitions. Write the correct form of the words in bold to complete the sentences.

> **careless** (adj) done, made, or said without paying attention
> **customer** (n) someone who buys goods or services from a business
> **goal** (n) something you want to do successfully in the future
> **messy** (adj) untidy or dirty
> **skill** (n) the ability to do an activity or job well
> **strength** (n) a good quality or ability that makes someone good at something
> **stress** (n) feelings of worry caused by problems
> **weakness** (n) a quality of someone or something that is not good

1 My business _____ for next year is to build a new factory.
2 I share an office with a colleague, so we both make sure our desks are not _____ . It would be hard to work if things were not neat and clean.
3 The business was failing, so the owners looked for some _____ in their business plan. They wanted to find out what the problem was so they could fix it.
4 Understanding a foreign language is an important _____ in business these days.
5 The salesperson was very pleased when the _____ put in a large order. It was a successful day for the business.
6 When you go for a job interview, you should talk about your _____ to show the interviewer you are the best person to hire.
7 I was trying to work quickly, and without thinking I made a _____ mistake. I ruined my entire project when I pushed the wrong button.
8 Ruining my project made me feel a lot of _____ . I had to do yoga after work to relax.

2 You are going to listen to a conversation between Joe, a business consultant, and Sam, a business owner. Discuss the questions in pairs.

1 Look at the photo. Which person is the consultant? Give reasons.
2 What skills do you think you need to be a business consultant? Do you think you would be good at it? Why or why not?
3 Why would a business owner need advice from a consultant?

WHILE LISTENING

3 ▶ 6.3 Listen to the conversation. Complete Sam's notes about advice that the consultant gives him.

Advice for Business

Problem: Workers are not (1)_____ at work – they don't work hard

Solutions: (2)_____ once a month

(3)_____ a brighter color

Result: Workers will be happier, work harder

Problem: Need to cut costs; spending too much money

Solution: Use less electricity; (4)_____ parts

Result: Make a better (5)_____

Problem: Having trouble reaching new customers

Solution: Add (6)_____

Result: Get new customers

Problem: Messy website – all black, hard to use

Solution: Hire a (7)_____

Color important: Use blue in website – many (8)_____ like it;
men, too

Website needs to be really (9)_____ and (10)_____ to use

Result: Get more online sales, more women will buy product

---

4 ▶ **6.4** Listen to the first part of the conversation again and number the phrases in the order you hear them.

a Was it useful _____
b Exactly! But there are things _____
c Oh, yeah _____
d Well, when we looked at the company's strengths and weaknesses _____
e Why are you stressed about that _____
f Useful ... Yeah, it was _____

5 Work with a partner. Decide which of the sentences in Exercise 4 look like statements and which sentences look like questions.

6 ▶ **6.5** Listen to a sentence from Exercise 4. Does it sound like a statement or a question? Why?

7 ▶ **6.6** Listen to the sentences in Exercise 4 again and repeat.

POST-LISTENING

8 Work with a partner. Use the notes from Exercise 3 to answer the questions.

1 What do you think Sam and the consultant discussed in their meeting before this one? How do you know?
2 Do you think Sam and the consultant will meet again? If so, what will they do in the next meeting?

DISCUSSION

9 Work with a partner. Use your notes from Listening 1 and Listening 2 to answer the questions.

1 What types of advice can a business get from a consultant?
2 What do you think is the most important thing for a business to do in order to make money? Why?
3 If you had a business with workers who didn't work hard, what would you do? Why?

SPEAKING

CRITICAL THINKING

At the end of this unit, you are going to do the Speaking Task below.

> Give advice to a failing business.

SKILLS

Using problem and solution charts

Use a problem and solution chart to help you organize your ideas when you give advice about a problem. This can also help you think about the outcome of a solution.

1 Work with a partner. What advice does the consultant give to the business owner in Listening 2? Match the possible solutions from the box to the problems in the chart.

REMEMBER ▲

> **a** Turn off the lights and computers at the end of the day; find cheaper parts for the products you make.
> **b** Add online sales.
> **c** Use colors that more women and men like.
> **d** ~~Organize social events and paint the office walls brighter colors.~~
> **e** Hire a professional web designer to create a nicer website that is easier to use.

problems	possible solutions	possible results
The employees are unhappy and don't work hard.	→ 1 _____d_____ →	Employees will be happier and work harder.
The company spends too much money on electricity and parts for the products they make.	→ 2 _____ →	
The business isn't getting new customers.	→ 3 _____ →	
The business has an old, messy website.	→ 4 _____ →	
The business wants to market more to women.	→ 5 _____ →	

2 What are some possible results of the solutions in Exercise 1? Look back at your notes from Listening 2, Exercise 3, and complete the *possible results* column in the chart.

3 With your partner, choose one of the businesses below. You will discuss this business in the Speaking Task at the end of this unit.

THE WAKE-UP CAFÉ

A small coffee shop just opened in a business area of a big city. The shop is open from 12 p.m. until 5 p.m. every day. The shop has no tables or chairs because the owner wants people to leave after they buy their coffee. The owner also buys expensive coffee beans because they are the most popular kind of coffee bean in the city. However, the owner complains that he is not getting enough customers and he is losing a lot of money very quickly. He might have to close the business next month if he keeps losing money and if more customers don't start coming into the shop.

DELIVERY RABBIT

A delivery company in a big city is not getting enough customers. Customers complain that the website is ugly and too hard to use, so they give up and choose other delivery companies. They also say that the deliveries are always late. The business has one delivery person who rides a bike. The business is losing a lot of money and might have to close if it doesn't get more customers soon.

FRESH FOOD MARKET

A grocery store in a small town is losing a lot of money. Customers complain that it is too dirty and that the food is never fresh. Another grocery store opened recently and is taking all of Fresh Food Market's customers. If the grocery store doesn't get its customers back, it will close next month.

4 Think about the business you chose in Exercise 3. Write three or four possible problems in the problem and solution chart.

business name: _____

	problems		possible solutions		possible results
1		→		→	
2		→		→	
3		→		→	
4		→		→	

5 Think about possible solutions for each problem. Use the advice from Listening 1 and Listening 2 and your own ideas to think of solutions and their possible results. Add your ideas to the problem and solution chart.

PREPARATION FOR SPEAKING

GIVING ADVICE

SKILLS

You can use certain phrases to introduce advice at the beginning of a sentence. The second part of the sentence gives advice.

If you want to sell more, you should start by trying to improve your advertising.

Here are some key phrases you can use to introduce advice:

I can help you.	Should we ... ?
I think you should ...	Why don't you ... ?
Be careful not to ...	If I were you, I would ...
Do you want to ... ?	If you want to ... , you should ...

1 Work with a partner. Look at the picture of a store. Think of reasons why the store might be having trouble with its business.

PRISM | Online Workbook

2 Work with a partner. Complete the sentences to give advice to the business in Exercise 1.

1 If I were you, I would …

_____ .

2 I think you should …

_____ .

3 If you want to do better, you should …

_____ .

4 Be careful not to …

_____ .

5 You should try (not) to …

_____ .

3 Read a conversation between the business owner and his business consultant. Underline the advice that the consultant gives. There is also one piece of inferred advice. What is it?

Consultant: I think you should try to improve your store.

Business owner: Oh. Can you give an example of how?

Consultant: Yeah. I don't want to upset you, but your store doesn't seem very attractive at the moment. It's a little messy in some places.

Business owner: OK. I see what you're saying. I'll work on that and make the store cleaner and neater.

Consultant: And if you want to bring in more customers, you need to have a more interesting front window.

Business owner: Do I? That's not really one of my strengths.

Consultant: I know it's difficult. I think you should hire a window designer. Then at least you know it will look nice.

Business owner: OK, great. I appreciate all of your advice.

4 Work with a partner. Student A: turn to page 191. Student B: turn to page 192. Follow the directions.

5 Imagine you are a business consultant. Work in a group of three. Make a list of ten dos and don'ts for small businesses.

6 Find someone from another group and take turns giving advice.

Give advice to a failing business.

PREPARE

1 Look back at the business you chose and the problem and solution chart in Critical Thinking. Add any new information.

2 Write a sentence to introduce advice for each problem. Use your notes in the *possible solutions* column in the chart from Critical Thinking and language from Preparation for Speaking.

1 _____

2 _____

3 _____

4 _____

3 Refer to the Task Checklist below as you prepare for your discussion.

TASK CHECKLIST	✔
Say numbers correctly.	
Use comparatives correctly.	
Use phrasal verbs correctly.	
Use phrases for giving advice.	

DISCUSS

4 Work with a new partner who chose a different business. Follow these steps as you discuss:

1 **Student A:** You are the owner of the business that Student B (the consultant) chose. Read the case study for the business that Student B will give advice for.

2 **Student B:** Give advice to Student A on how he or she can solve the problems for the business. Describe possible results for each solution.

3 **Student A:** Take notes on Student B's advice. Which piece of advice do you think will be the most helpful? Why?

4 Switch roles and repeat.

ON CAMPUS

PREPARING TO LISTEN

1 Work in small groups. Discuss the questions.

1 Do you like working in groups, or do you prefer to work alone?
2 Have you ever worked on a group project for a class? Describe the experience.
3 Group projects are very common in North American universities. Why do you think this is true?

2 Read the list of advantages and disadvantages of group work. Write *A* (advantage) or *D* (disadvantage) next to each point.

1 Students participate actively in learning. _____
2 Groups may need a lot of time to organize and plan the work. _____
3 Students can learn from each other. _____
4 Working in teams can prepare students for work in the future. _____
5 There are a lot of meetings. _____
6 Students must find a time and place for everyone to meet. _____
7 Students can make friends with others in the group. _____
8 One or two people often do most of the work. _____

3 Compare your answers. Can you add any more advantages or disadvantages?

WHILE LISTENING

4 ▶ 6.7 You are going to hear two students describe their experience of group work. Listen and circle whether the experience was positive or negative.

Alex: *positive / negative*   **Yuki:** *positive / negative*

5 ▶ 6.7 Look back at the list in Exercise 2. Then listen again. Which of the points do Alex and Yuki mention? Write the numbers.

Alex: _____ , _____ , _____
Yuki: _____ , _____ , _____

6 Work with a partner. Discuss the questions.

1 Have you experienced situations like the ones that Alex and Yuki describe?
2 Read the information in the box. Which strategies could help solve the problems that Yuki mentioned?

SKILLS

Strategies for group projects

- Have a clear goal.
- Choose a leader.
- Plan a timeline, with deadlines for each part of the project.
- Make sure that every member of the group has a specific task.
- Respect everyone's point of view.

PRACTICE

7 Look at the quotes. Match each quote to one of the strategies in the box.

> **1** What do you think about this, Amina?
> _Respect everyone's point of view._

> **4** We should try to finish this by Friday. Then next week we can …
> _____

> **2** I can do this part of the project. Would you like to take charge of … ?
> _____

> **5** Let's choose a leader. I'd like to nominate Cheng.
> _____

> **3** Let's focus on what we need to do today.
> _____

REAL-WORLD APPLICATION

8 Work in small groups. Choose one of the tasks below to do as a group. You will present your project to the class in two weeks. Hold a planning meeting. Work out a timeline and a schedule, and assign specific roles to each person.

- Create a website, wiki, or blog for your class.
- Write a short comedy sketch to be presented to the class.
- Create a short audio or video news program about events in your school and/or in your town or city.

9 Report back to the class. Answer the questions.

1 What exactly is your group going to produce?
2 What is each person in the group going to do?
3 How are you going to organize your time?
4 Did your group work well together? Why or why not?

LEARNING OBJECTIVES

Listening skill	Listen for attitude
Pronunciation	Intonation for emotion and interest
Speaking skills	Time order; examples and details
Speaking Task	Give a presentation about a remarkable person and his or her work
On Campus	Give presentations

ACTIVATE YOUR KNOWLEDGE

Work with a partner. Look at the photo and answer the questions.

1 Some people are extraordinary. They do very special, unusual, or strange things. Do you know anyone like this?

2 Why is the person in the photo extraordinary? What kind of personality do extraordinary people have?

3 What extraordinary thing would you like to do?

PREPARING TO WATCH

1 Work with a partner and answer the questions.

1 Where in the world is Kenya?
2 What ocean is to the east of Kenya?
3 What can you find on a beach?

2 Work with a partner. Look at the photos from the video and read the newspaper headline. Then answer the questions.

Kiwayu People Earn Money from the Beach

1 What do you see on the beach?
2 What are the people doing in the photos?
3 How do you think the people of Kiwayu make money?

GLOSSARY

flip-flop (n) a kind of open shoe that people often wear at the beach

isolated (adj) very far from other places

ornament (n) an object that decorates a home or yard

trash (n) the things you throw away because you do not want them; garbage

wash up (phr v) to move something naturally from the water to the beach

---

WHILE WATCHING

3 ▶ Watch the video. Circle the correct answers.

UNDERSTANDING
MAIN IDEAS

1 There *are / are not* a lot of tourists on the beaches of Kiwayu Island.
2 The people who live there seem *connected to / isolated from* the rest of the world.
3 Trash from *the ocean / people who live there* is on the beach.
4 People pick up trash on the beach *weekly / daily* to earn a living.
5 People turn the trash into *flip-flops / art*.
6 They *make / don't make* money from the tourists.
7 They send *some / most* of their ornaments to Nairobi, Kenya.
8 These ornaments are sold to stores around the *country / world*.

4 ▶ Watch again. Work with a partner. Match the questions and answers.

UNDERSTANDING
DETAILS

1 Where do people sell the ornaments?   **a** flip-flops
2 Who goes to the beach to pick up trash?   **b** some of their children
3 What do people collect on the beach?   **c** houses
4 Where do they take the trash to?   **d** artists and craftsmen
5 Who turns the trash into ornaments?   **e** Kiwayu women
6 What do the people of Kiwayu make?   **f** money
7 What did Kiwayu people not have before?   **g** on the Internet
8 Who could not go to school before?   **h** the Kiwayu villages

5 Work with a partner. Why does the woman in the video say that education is the most important thing? Circle the best reason.

MAKING INFERENCES

a Children can learn to pick up plastic and other trash.
b Staying at home on an island is boring to children.
c Children can have a better future.

DISCUSSION

6 Work with a partner. Discuss the questions.

1 How can we stop people from putting trash into the oceans?
2 Do you think turning trash into art is a good idea? Why or why not?
3 What do artists and craftsmen in your country make for tourists?

7 Work in small groups. Imagine you are artists in Kiwayu. Look in the box at the things that wash up on the beach. What could you make from each one?

| bottle caps   boxes   glass bottles   paper bags |
| plastic bags   plastic cups   tires   soda cans |

LISTENING

LISTENING 1

PREPARING TO LISTEN

UNDERSTANDING KEY VOCABULARY

1 You are going to listen to a student presentation about creative people and the things they make. Read the sentences. Choose the best definitions for the words in bold.

1 I like the **design** of the new building in town. It has space for business as well as for relaxation.
   a the way something is planned and made
   b the parts of something that are needed

2 A spoon is very **simple**. It doesn't have any moving parts and doesn't use electricity.
   a not difficult or complicated; without extra things that are not needed
   b cheap to buy

3 A car is a **complicated** machine. It has many parts. Also, it takes time to learn to drive one.
   a having a lot of different pieces, in a way that is difficult to understand
   b valuable

4 Salt has many **uses**. It can be used to cook and clean, and it even has medical uses.
   a things you must or should have
   b reasons why something is used

5 Sara's new painting was so beautiful that she won a prize for her **achievement** in art.
   a money you win
   b something good and successful that you do, usually by working hard

6 Each part of your office chair has a **purpose**. The armrests on your chair hold up your arms so that your wrists are comfortable when you type.
   a the way something is made
   b why you do something or why something is present

7 When you give a presentation, you should have a few main **points**, like why something is important or how something helps people.
   a opinions, facts, or ideas that are said or written
   b the sharp end of a needle

8 What do you think is the best **invention** ever made by someone trying to solve a problem – the phone, the computer, or the car?
   a something made for the first time
   b an expensive item

2 Discuss the questions in pairs.

1 Who are some inventors or designers that you know of?
2 What were their inventions or designs?
3 How did their inventions or designs change lives?

WHILE LISTENING

3 ▶ 7.1 Listen and write the name of the person and the object under the correct photo. One person is used twice.

object	person
hand-dryer	James Dyson
egg chair	Sir Jonathan Ive
wheelbarrow	Arne Jacobsen
iPhone	

a

b

_____

_____

c

d

_____

_____

4 ▶ 7.1 Read the student's notes. Then listen again and complete the information. Compare your answers with a partner.

inventor/designer and interesting points	inventions/designs and achievements	why the person is important
Arne Jacobsen Hard worker, Liked to joke, (1)_____ relaxed him	Chair: (2)_____ and neat design, his designs still used today → he worked to make them perfect	Was famous for (3)_____, simple designs of furniture and buildings; he thought about the (4)_____ his designs would serve for people
James Dyson Studied (5)_____, design, and engineering; Still likes art – made waterfall with water going up, not down	Inventions include: wheelbarrow with round wheel, hand-dryer, vacuum cleaner Supports education, research, and gives money so (7)_____ will become inventors, too	Inventions made to solve (6)_____ Gets ideas because he sees things that can work better Dyson is still (8)_____ new things
Sir Jonathan Ive Named Knight Commander of the British Empire in 2013 Hardworking and (9)_____	Designed many products for Apple, which are (10)_____, clean, and thin	Ive has won a lot of (11)_____ for his designs Lots of people know and use products he designed

DISCUSSION

5 Discuss the questions in small groups.

1 Which of the inventors or designers do you think is the most interesting? Why?
2 How do designers and inventors help improve life for people?
3 What "ordinary" things that we use often are actually special and help us?

⊙ LANGUAGE DEVELOPMENT

ADJECTIVE ENDINGS

LANGUAGE

-ed and -ing

Many adjectives end in -ed or -ing. Some have both endings. These endings change the meaning of the adjective.

You can often change a word to an adjective by adding -ed or -ing.
relax (v) → **relaxed** (adj) / **relaxing** (adj)
surprise (n/v) → **surprised** (adj) / **surprising** (adj)
(Note: Remove the final -e in surprise.)

Adjectives that end in -ing describe the reason for a feeling (e.g., a situation or thing).
Stories about accidental inventions, like Post-It Notes®, are really **interesting**.
Stories about really simple inventions, like paper straws, are pretty **boring**.

Adjectives that end in -ed describe what people feel as a result of something.
Sarah is **interested** in the inventor Thomas Edison.
I get **bored** when my Internet connection isn't working.

1 Look at the sentences from Listening 1. Underline the adjectives.

1 It's really amazing.
2 He found painting to be relaxing.
3 He got frustrated and worked to improve it.
4 But he is also interested in supporting education.

PRISM Online Workbook

2 Compare the two sentences. Underline the word that the adjective describes in each sentence.

    1 **a** The news was surprising.
          b I was surprised by the news.
    2 **a** I was always bored when I went to visit her.
          b She was boring, so I tried not to visit her.
    3 **a** He was excited by the idea for the new invention.
          b His idea for the new invention was exciting.
    4 **a** My mom was very interested in my story.
          b My mom told me a very interesting story.
    5 **a** The walk was very tiring.
          b The walk took a long time because I was tired.
    6 **a** What a fascinating idea!
          b My friend was fascinated by the idea, but I didn't like it.

3 Write the correct form of the words in parentheses to complete the text. Use the *-ed* or *-ing* form to make adjectives.

J oseph Conrad was born in 1857 in Ukraine. His father was a writer and translator of famous books and plays. Joseph read these books and became
(1)_____ (fascinate) with literature. Joseph's family was rich, but he didn't have a very
(2)_____ (excite) childhood. Because of his parents' political beliefs, he and his family had to move to northern Russia, where life was very hard. Both of Joseph's parents died when he was only 12 years old. But then there was a (3)_____ (surprise) change in his life. Joseph's uncle decided to care for him and pay for his education in Latin, Greek, geography, and mathematics. Unfortunately, Joseph thought studying was (4)_____ (bore). So he told his uncle that he was (5)_____ (tire) of studying and wanted to become a sailor and travel to Africa by ship. While he was a sailor, Joseph enjoyed having adventures at sea and meeting lots of (6)_____ (interest) people. These people were later included in his books. After he stopped sailing, he wrote many books and became one of the most successful 20th-century writers. Perhaps his most famous book is *Heart of Darkness*, which has been made into movies and even used as the idea for a video game. One of the reasons Conrad's books were popular was that the characters in the books he wrote were very believable.

4 Work with a partner. Check your answers.

THE PAST PROGRESSIVE

LANGUAGE

Forming the past progressive

Use the past progressive to describe actions that were in progress at a specific time in the past.

For affirmative statements, use *was/were* + verb + *-ing*.
He **was studying** math last spring.
They **were doing** research for their presentation before class.

For negative statements, use *was/were* + *not* + verb + *-ing*.
He **was not / wasn't trying** to invent the potato chip, but he did.
They **were not / weren't working** at the time.

Use the contractions *wasn't / weren't* in everyday speaking. The full forms, *was not* and *were not*, are more common in formal writing.

PRISM Online Workbook

5 Write the past progressive form of the verb in parentheses to complete the sentences.

1 Last year I _____ (go) to school part-time.
2 John _____ (work) part-time at a supermarket in 2002.
3 In 2014 my sister and I _____ (live) in Tokyo.
4 We _____ (not / study) last night.
  We _____ (cook) dinner.
5 At 6 p.m. yesterday my friends _____ (travel) to Dubai on a plane.
6 On the Fourth of July, Marco _____ (prepare) a lot of delicious food for a picnic.
7 Last night Peishan _____ (think) a lot about her family in Shanghai.
8 Maria _____ (not / live) in Guatemala last year.

The past progressive and the simple past

Use the past progressive for an action in progress in the past. Use the simple past for an action that happened one time or was completed.

He **was studying** for the exam last night.

He **passed** the exam.

Use *when* or *while* in a past progressive time clause to show an event that was in progress when a second event happened. Use the simple past in the main clause.

time clause – event in progress   *main clause – second event*

When/While he was working on his invention, he decided to go to college.

main clause – second event   *time clause – event in progress*

He decided to go to college **when/while he was working on his invention**.

Use *when*, but not *while*, in a simple past time clause to show an event that happened while an event was already in progress. Use the past progressive in the main clause.

main clause – event in progress   *time clause – second event*

We were presenting our project in class when the fire alarm went off.

time clause – second event   *main clause – event in progress*

When the fire alarm went off, **we were presenting our project in class**.

6 Write the past progressive or the simple past form of the verbs to complete the paragraph.

Throughout history, people have accidentally invented some amazing things. For example, in 1945, Percy Spencer, an American engineer, (1)_____ (work) in a lab. One day while he (2)_____ (do) an experiment with vacuum tubes inside radars, something amazing (3)_____ (happen). While he (4)_____ (watch) the experiment heat up, he (5)_____ (realize) that a candy bar in his pocket had melted. Spencer (6)_____ (be) very surprised. However, his coworkers (7)_____ (not / believe) him. He (8)_____ (decide) to try the experiment again with other foods to see if they would cook, too. The next day he (9)_____ (bring) an egg to the lab. When one coworker (10)_____ (look) over the microwave experiment, the egg (11)_____ (blow) up in his face. Spencer accidentally (12)_____ (invent) the microwave oven.

7 Write *when* or *while* to complete the sentences. In some items, more than one answer is possible.

1 _____ he was studying in college, he didn't work as an inventor.
2 _____ the German scientist Wilhelm Röntgen was doing an experiment, he accidentally discovered X-rays.
3 I was reading about Joseph Conrad _____ the phone rang.
4 William Kellogg accidentally created Corn Flakes cereal _____ he was searching for healthy, vegetarian food.
5 Monique was working at Apple _____ Steve Jobs was the CEO.
6 We were in the meeting room _____ the lights went out.
7 Alison was working on her new project _____ her mother came to the door.
8 _____ Jessica and Maria were walking to class, they saw a hawk fly over them.

Wilhelm Röntgen and his X-ray machine

PRISM Online Workbook

PREPARING TO LISTEN

1 You are going to listen to a conversation between students who are preparing for a presentation on interesting people. Read the sentences. Write the words in bold next to the definitions.

1 Albert Einstein was a **remarkable** man. He was an extremely intelligent person and did many important things in math and physics.

2 Percy Spencer had a lot of **success** when he invented the microwave oven. Almost everyone has a microwave oven now.

3 Something **amazing** happened in 2013 – in South America someone discovered a new species. People were shocked because it had been 35 years since the last new animal was found.

4 Alex is a young **entrepreneur**. He created his own business when he was only 16 years old.

5 Conrad was in a difficult **situation** as a child because both of his parents died.

6 After Joseph Conrad **retired** from being a sailor and didn't work anymore, he used his free time to write books.

a _____ (v) to leave your job and stop working, usually because you get older

b _____ (adj) very surprising

c _____ (adj) very unusual or noticeable in a way that you admire

d _____ (n) the things that are happening and are present at a particular time and place

e _____ (n) someone who starts his or her own business

f _____ (n) something that has a good result

Jonathan Koon

2 Discuss the questions in pairs.

1 What kind of life do you think a young entrepreneur has? Think about his or her job, family, and interests.

2 Can anyone become an entrepreneur at a young age? Why?

WHILE LISTENING

3 ▶ 7.2 Listen to the students' conversation. Take notes about the people they discuss. Be sure to note who the people are, their jobs, and the things they did that are remarkable.

SKILLS

Listening for attitude

When people speak they don't always say what they think directly. If they don't want to sound negative, they use a positive adjective with a negative verb, e.g., *It isn't very good* instead of *It's bad.* They also weaken a negative statement by using phrases like *a little.* Being aware of this when listening can help you understand what the speaker really means.

4 Answer the questions. Use your notes to help you.

1 What work do Luisa and Yasmin have to do? _____

_____

2 Who has done most of their work? _____

5 ▶ 7.2 Listen again and write words to complete what Luisa says.

1 Actually, I'm _____ great.
2 Well ... I haven't done _____ .
3 I'm _____ at finding things to present.
4 I don't know _____ Conrad.

6 Decide who says the sentences. Write *L* (Luisa) or *Y* (Yasmin).

1 I'm having trouble doing it. _____
2 The introduction's not great. _____
3 It needs a little more work. _____
4 His life doesn't sound that extraordinary. _____
5 Well, I'm not sure I understand everything. _____

7 Write three facts about Jonathan Koon and Joseph Conrad. Use your notes from Exercise 3 to help you.

Jonathan Koon

1 _____

2 _____

3 _____

Joseph Conrad

4 _____

5 _____

6 _____

8 Read the *Listening for attitude* box on page 159 again. Match the sentences in Exercise 5 to the two ways of sounding less negative.

A: Use a positive adjective with a negative verb.
B: Weaken a negative statement by using phrases.

9 Luisa does not always say what she thinks directly. Choose the correct word in each sentence that shows what Luisa really thinks.

1 Luisa is feeling *good / bad.*
2 Luisa *has prepared / hasn't prepared* her presentation.
3 Luisa is *good / bad* at finding out things to present.
4 Luisa *knows / doesn't know* about Joseph Conrad.

PRONUNCIATION FOR LISTENING

> **SKILLS**
>
> **Intonation for emotion and interest**
>
> When people speak, they show different levels of interest by changing the sound of their voice.
>
> When speakers are enthusiastic, their voice goes up. Or they may say the word that shows their emotion louder.
>
> That's remárkable!
>
> When speakers are unenthusiastic, their voice stays flat or drops down. Or they may say the word that shows their emotion more quietly.
>
> I'm not so good.

10 ▶ 7.3 Listen to the sentences. Check (✔) the sentences that sound enthusiastic.

1 I am pretty happy with it. ☐
2 He's a remarkable man. ☐
3 That's amazing! ☐
4 I'll check him out. ☐

11 Work with a partner. Take turns saying the sentences aloud. Ask your partner if you sound enthusiastic or not.

1 That's good.
2 She's interesting.
3 The weather is fantastic.
4 I'm happy with my work.

DISCUSSION

12 Work in small groups. Think of other people who did or did not have money or power but did something extraordinary.

13 Use your notes from Listening 1 and Listening 2 to discuss the questions in small groups.

1 What makes a person remarkable or amazing? Give examples from Listening 1 and Listening 2.
2 What do you think would make a person's life boring to hear about?
3 What are the benefits of the work done or inventions made by the people discussed in Listening 1 and Listening 2?

SYNTHESIZING

SPEAKING

CRITICAL THINKING

At the end of this unit, you are going to do the Speaking Task below.

> Give a presentation about a remarkable person and his or her work. Describe the impact of this person's work on our lives.

SKILLS

Using an idea map

Use an idea map to think of topics and related subtopics that you want to find information about. Start with your main topic in the center of the idea map. Write subtopics on the "legs" of the idea map. Use the map to help you do research about your topic and subtopics and organize the information that you find.

 REMEMBER

1 Work with a partner. Fill in the idea map about Jonathan Koon. Use your notes from Exercise 3 in Listening 2 (page 159) to help you. Write the letter of each phrase in the bubbles.

a invented a cell phone holder
b bought a clothing brand in 2008 from JayZ
c parents from Hong Kong
d designed clothing with an Italian designer
e egg-shaped piece sold for thousands
f born in U.S. in 1983

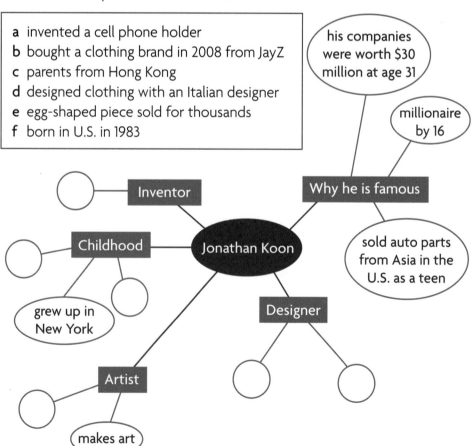

2 Now think about a remarkable person you would like to find out about. You will do a presentation about this person in the Speaking Task at the end of this unit.

3 Go online and do research about the person. Create an idea map about the person to organize your ideas.

PREPARATION FOR SPEAKING

TIME ORDER

When you describe events in someone's life, use words or phrases that help show the order of events. Here are some examples of words or phrases that show time order:

first of all, in (year), at that time, when, by the time, before, then, after (that), nowadays

When you hear these expressions, you can understand when events happened in relation to one another.

1 Write time order expressions to complete the paragraph. In some items, more than one answer is possible.

PRISM Online Workbook

(1)_____ many people know about chocolate chip cookies. But (2)_____ 1930, no one had tasted one. (3)_____ Ruth Graves Wakefield was cooking for the inn that she owned with her husband. One day Ms. Wakefield tried to make a chocolate cookie by chopping up a chocolate bar and (4)_____ , mixing it into her cookie dough. (5)_____ she baked the cookies, the chocolate didn't melt like the chocolate she usually used. Instead the chocolate was just in pieces in the cookies. Ms. Wakefield's guests loved the cookies, though. (6)_____ her chocolate chip cookies became very popular, and people still eat cookies using the same recipe today.

EXAMPLES AND DETAILS

Introducing examples and details to support a presentation

When you give a presentation, it is important to give details and examples. This makes your main ideas easier to understand and more interesting to your audience. You can use these phrases to introduce details and examples:

For example, ...
One example ... / Another example, ... / An important example ...
Equally important ...
such as ... / also ...

2 ▶ 7.4 Listen to the student's presentation. Write the phrases that the student uses to introduce examples and details.

My presentation is about Thomas Edison. He was an American inventor, and he was born in 1847. He is a remarkable person because he invented a lot of the things we know and use every day, (1)_____ the electric light bulb. Well, he wasn't the first to invent one, but he *was* the first person to invent one that could last a long time. This was in 1879 while he was working in his research lab in Menlo Park, New Jersey. It lasted 14.5 hours! (2)_____ of Edison's amazing inventions is the motion picture camera. We all know this today as the video camera. Edison and his team invented it in 1891, and they showed short, six-minute movies. (3)_____ was Edison's work with Henry Ford, who started the Ford Motor Company. Edison was worried about America's dependence on foreign rubber for tires. So while he was working at a lab in Florida in 1927, he found a new source of rubber in local plants ...

3 Work with a partner. Take turns reading the presentation aloud. What other phrases could you use in Exercise 2?

> Give a presentation about a remarkable person and his or her work.
> Describe the impact of this person's work on our lives.

PRISM Online Workbook

PREPARE

1 Look back at the idea map you created in Critical Thinking. Add any new information you would like to include.

2 Look at the subtopics in your idea map. Write sentences you can use to introduce them in your presentation. Use language from Preparation for Speaking to help you.

_____

_____

_____

_____

3 Refer to the Task Checklist below as you prepare your presentation.

TASK CHECKLIST	✔
Use words and intonation to sound less negative and more positive.	
Use -ed and -ing adjectives correctly.	
Use time order expressions to show the order in which events took place.	
Use the past progressive correctly.	
Give details and examples about the person and his or her work.	

PRESENT

4 Work in small groups. Take turns presenting your person to your group.

ON CAMPUS

GIVING PRESENTATIONS

PREPARING TO LISTEN

1 How do you feel about speaking English in these situations? Check (✔) one of the boxes.

	very nervous	a little nervous	OK	I enjoy it!
chatting with classmates before class				
talking to people you don't know				
answering a teacher's question in class				
participating in a group discussion				
giving a presentation to the class				

2 Work in small groups and compare your answers.

WHILE LISTENING

3 ▶ 7.5 Listen to a professor talk about giving presentations in class. In column A, write the three things students should do to prepare for a presentation.

A What should you do?	B How should you do it?
1	
2	
3	

4 ▶ 7.5 Listen again. In column B, write the professor's suggestions for how students can prepare for a presentation.

5 Work with a partner and compare your notes. Answer the questions.

1 Have you used any of the strategies that the professor recommends? Which ones?

2 What other advice could you add?

Strategies for successful presentations

Practice your speech aloud several times beforehand.

Make eye contact with the audience.

Pronounce and stress important words, names, and numbers clearly.

Pause between your main points.

PRACTICE

6 Read these excerpts from a presentation about the history of Apple. Underline the key words and try to pronounce them.

1 Apple Computers was founded on April 1, 1976, by Steve Jobs and Steve Wozniak. They wanted to create a computer that people could use at home. They had very little money, so they worked in Steve Jobs's garage.

2 In 1977, Jobs and Wozniak created the Apple 1. It was the first personal computer, with a keyboard and a screen. They sold 200 units for $666 each.

3 The following year, they introduced the Apple II. It was a better design, and it was lighter than the Apple 1. It also had color graphics. This was a very successful product. Sales went from $7.8M in 1978 to $117M in 1980. Apple sold about 6 million units over 16 years. In 1980, Apple became a public company.

7 Work with a partner. Practice reading the excerpts aloud. Stress the key words, and pause after each point. Make eye contact with your partner.

REAL-WORLD APPLICATION

8 Read the notes for the rest of the presentation. Underline the key words. Choose a card. Present the information to a partner.

1983: Wozniak left Apple. Jobs replaced him with John Sculley BUT disagreements between Jobs and Sculley over management of company 1985: Jobs left Apple Founded NeXT (software company) Bought Pixar (animation company – made *Toy Story*, *Finding Nemo*, etc. Now owned by Disney)	1990s: Apple was not succeeding – losing customers 1997: Jobs returned to Apple. Then introduced several new products: • iMac (1998) • iPod – MP3 player (2001) • iPhone – most popular (2007) • iPad (2010)

9 After each mini-presentation, ask your partner these questions:

1 Was the information clear? Was it easy to understand?

2 Was the speech too fast, too slow, or just right?

LEARNING OBJECTIVES

Listening skill	Understand meaning from context
Pronunciation	Words with easily confused sounds
Speaking skills	Turn-taking; show levels of agreement
Speaking Task	Discuss how to get children interested in space exploration
On Campus	Review for exams

ACTIVATE YOUR KNOWLEDGE

Work with a partner. Look at the photo and answer the questions.

1 What does the photo show?
2 What types of things can we learn from studying the night sky?
3 Do you think we should spend a lot of money on space exploration? Why or why not?

WATCH AND LISTEN

PREPARING TO WATCH

ACTIVATING YOUR KNOWLEDGE

1 Work with a partner and answer the questions.

1 What are the names of the eight planets in our solar system?
2 What else is there in space?
3 Do you think learning about space is important? Why or why not?

PREDICTING CONTENT USING VISUALS

2 You are going to watch a video about the Voyager space project. Look at the pictures from the video. What are the people doing?

> **GLOSSARY**
>
> **dish** (n) a round piece of equipment that receives information from objects in space
>
> **NASA** (n) the U.S. government organization that plans and controls space travel and studies space
>
> **solar system** (n) the sun and the planets, such as Earth and Saturn, that move around it
>
> **speed of light** (n) how fast light moves (about 300 million meters per second)

WHILE WATCHING

UNDERSTANDING DETAILS

3 ▶ Watch the video. Complete each sentence with a number or word from the box. Check your answers with a partner.

> 11   17   1977   2012   space   years

1 Voyager began its journey in _____ .
2 Almost 40 _____ later, Voyager still communicates with a dish.
3 It communicates with this dish over _____ billion miles away.
4 In _____ , Voyager left our solar system.
5 Voyager's message takes more than _____ hours to get to Earth.
6 The little green triangle shows Voyager in deep _____ .

4 Read the questions and circle the correct answer.

   1 Where does NASA communicate with Voyager?
     a The Mojave Desert in California   **b** Kennedy Space Station in Texas

   2 Who is the scientist for the Voyager project?
     a Dr. Edmund Halley   **b** Dr. Edward Stone

   3 What planets did Voyager fly by?
     a Mars, Venus, and Mercury   **b** Jupiter, Saturn, Uranus,
                                         and Neptune

   4 How fast does a message travel from Voyager to the dish?
     a at the speed of light   **b** at the speed of sound

   5 Where did Voyager 1 become the first man-made object to ever travel to?
     a outside the solar system   **b** inside the solar system

5 ▶ Watch again and check your answers to Exercise 4.

6 Work with a partner. Discuss the questions.

   1 What was Voyager's goal when it flew by the planets?
   2 What is NASA learning from Voyager?
   3 Did the Voyager team know how long Voyager could survive?

DISCUSSION

7 Work in small groups. Discuss the questions.

   1 What are some things we learn from space organizations like NASA?
   2 Do you think working for NASA would be exciting? Why or why not?
   3 Why might it be difficult to work for NASA?

8 Look in the box at the ways to send messages. Then answer the questions.

> by phone   by mail   by text   by email

   1 What is the fastest way to send a message? What's the slowest way?
   2 How do you know when someone gets your message?
   3 Can messages be saved or deleted for each way? How?
   4 Which way do you prefer to send messages? Why?

LISTENING

LISTENING 1

PRONUNCIATION FOR LISTENING
WORDS WITH EASILY CONFUSED SOUNDS

1 ▶ 8.1 Listen to the sentences. Underline two words in each sentence that sound the same.

1 When the sun is out, I make sure my son uses sunscreen so he doesn't get sunburned.
2 Have you read the information about the Red Planet?
3 We are having a picnic whether it is hot or not. It has been good weather recently, so we are hoping it will be nice.
4 She ate her dinner before she went out at eight o'clock.
5 There are two doctors in the family, and their daughter is also studying medicine.
6 Our guest was in the house for an hour.

2 Work with a partner. Take turns saying the pairs of words aloud. What do you notice about the spelling and the sound of the words?

1   weather   whether
2   our   hour
3   sun   son
4   read   red
5   there   their
6   sent   scent
7   ate   eight
8   mined   mind
9   for   four
10 to   two

3 ▶ 8.2 Listen to the sentences that have some of the words in Exercise 2. Write down each sentence as you listen.

1 _____
2 _____
3 _____
4 _____
5 _____
6 _____

PREPARING TO LISTEN

4 You are going to listen to a radio program about space travel. Read the definitions. Write the correct form of the words in bold to complete the sentences.

> **beyond** (prep) on the other side of something
> **explore** (v) to travel around a place to find out what is there
> **journey** (n) a long trip from one place to another
> **path** (n) the direction that a person or thing moves in
> **planet** (n) a large, round object in space that moves around the sun or another star
> **reach** (v) to arrive somewhere
> **spacecraft** (n) a vehicle that can travel into space
> **surface** (n) the top or outside part of something

1 Scientists are trying to develop a _____ that can carry people all the way to Mars.

2 In our solar system, Earth is the only _____ humans can live on. Some people think that Mars could be a home for humans one day.

3 Researchers want to go deep into space and _____ other solar systems. There is a lot we could learn from research in space.

4 It takes about three days to travel at least 240,000 miles (386,400 km) from Earth to the moon. That's a long _____ .

5 Earth's _____ is made of large masses of land and large bodies of water.

6 Scientists hope to _____ Mars by the year 2030. Right now, only robots and satellites have arrived there.

7 The moon follows a _____ around Earth. Similarly, Earth follows one around the sun.

8 Scientists sent a satellite _____ our own solar system. We now have more information about places farther away from Earth.

WHILE LISTENING

Understanding meaning from context

Some words sound the same or very similar. If the words sound the same, you have to guess from the context which word is correct.

5 ▶ **8.3** Listen to the first part of the radio program. Complete the sentences with the words you hear.

1 We'll think about the planets people haven't visited yet and _____ we are likely to visit some of them in the future.

2 Let's begin inside our own solar system, which is made up of all the planets and the _____ .

3 Mars is known as the "_____ Planet" because of its color.

4 NASA, the U.S. government group that studies space, so far has only _____ robot explorers to Mars.

5 Even with the danger, many people want _____ travel to Mars.

6 Read the sentences in Exercise 5 again and check the spelling of the words you wrote.

TAKING NOTES ON DETAILS

7 ▶ **8.4** Listen to the second part of the radio program. Complete the student's outline.

I NASA plans to send people to asteroid
  A Send to asteroid by (1)_____ ; asteroid = very large rock goes around (2)_____
    1 Robot reaches asteroid and takes a large (3)_____
    2 Robot sends it on a path around (4)_____
    3 People (5)_____ asteroid in 2020s; travel on Orion spacecraft
  B Other uses for Orion
    1 No travel to Mars
    2 (6)_____ new spacecraft
II Lucy – BPM 37093
  A (7)_____ star = white dwarf star
    1 Doesn't burn, shines with (8)_____
    2 Huge diamond – bigger than all diamonds ever found on Earth
    3 (9)_____ our solar system
  B Facts about Lucy
    1 about (10)_____ miles (4,000 km) across
    2 smaller than Earth, but half as wide
    3 cold star, other stars much hotter
      a only half as (11)_____ as our sun

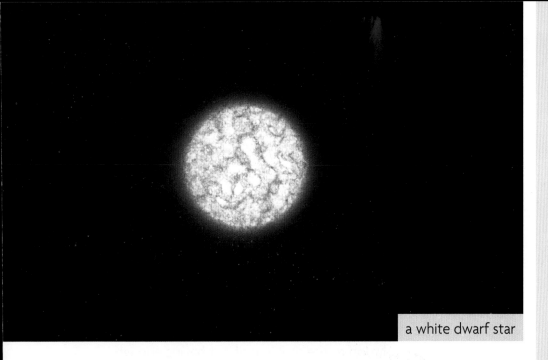

a white dwarf star

8 Write *T* (true) or *F* (false) next to the statements. Then correct the false statements.

_____ **1** NASA plans to have robots change an asteroid's path and send it around the moon.

_____

_____ **2** A human trip to Mars is planned for the 2020s.

_____

_____ **3** Dwarf stars are found in our solar system.

_____

_____ **4** Lucy is larger than Earth.

_____

_____ **5** Lucy is hotter than our sun.

_____

9 ▶ 8.4 Listen to the second part of the program again. Write down one more piece of information about NASA's plans for Mars exploration and one more piece of information about the dwarf star Lucy.

1 _____

2 _____

DISCUSSION

10 Discuss the questions with a partner.

1 What are some possible reasons why people want to go to Mars?

2 What would be some of the benefits of being able to go there?

3 What do you think about a robot bringing an asteroid boulder to orbit the moon? What could be dangerous about this?

VOCABULARY FOR PROBLEMS AND SOLUTIONS

1 Read the sentences. Write the words in bold to complete the table.

1 We will talk about the **issue** of paying for space exploration.

2 What is the **impact** of space exploration on people today? Does it make our lives better?

3 What **options** do we have for paying for things like going to Mars? Is there more than one way to pay?

4 One **alternative** to the government paying for space research is private companies doing it.

5 If we don't have enough money for space exploration, it is a **problem** because then scientists cannot continue the very important research they are doing.

6 It seems that a **solution** to the problem of not having enough money could be to tax the companies that make a profit from space exploration.

7 When people stay in space for a long time, what **effects** are there? Do they get sick more, or do they have trouble when they come back to Earth?

A word	B definition
a _option_	(n) a choice
b _effect_	(n) a change, reaction, or result that is caused by something
c _____	(n) the answer to the problem
d _____	(n) the effect that a person, event, or situation has on someone or something
e _____	(n) a situation that causes difficulties and needs to be solved
f _____	(n) an important topic or problem that people are discussing
g _____	(n) one of two or more things you can choose between

2 Which words in the table have similar meanings?

3 Complete the sentences with the words from Exercises 1 and 2. In some items, more than one answer is possible.

1 One _____ with going to Mars is that we don't have enough information about how to survive once we get there.

2 What is the _____ that we will discuss in class on Friday? I want to read more about it before then so that I have enough support for my ideas.

3 In the future, will there be a(n) _____ to travel to space as a tourist, or will only scientists be able to go?

4 What type of _____ would there be if we stopped exploring space? What do you think would happen?

5 There are about 500,000 pieces of space junk (old broken things in space) orbiting Earth that could harm a spacecraft. But the only _____ for a spacecraft to not get hit is to try to move out of the way of the junk.

6 I don't see any _____ to having governments pay for at least part of space research. Companies only want to pay for things that will make money, not for things that are just interesting to know.

7 What _____ does the moon have on people? Does a full moon cause things to happen on our planet or affect things in nature?

FUTURE UNREAL CONDITIONALS

LANGUAGE

Use *future unreal conditionals* to describe imagined situations in the future.

Use the simple past in the *if* clause to describe the imagined situation. Then use a modal in the main clause to describe the predicted result (*would*) or the possible outcome (*could*).

| *if clause* | *main clause – predicted result* |

If Lucy were mined, there would be more diamonds than on Earth.

| *main clause – predicted result* | *if clause* |

There would be more diamonds than on Earth if Lucy were mined.

The *if* clause can come before or after the main clause.

Notice that in the *if* clause, the past form *were* (*be*) is used for all persons (*I, you, we, they, he, she, it*).

| *if clause* | *main clause – possible outcome* |

If a very light spacesuit were invented, people could walk around on Mars easily.

| *main clause – possible outcome* | *if clause* |

People could walk around on Mars easily if a very light spacesuit were invented.

4 Complete the sentences using future unreal conditionals and the words in parentheses. Use *would* or *could* in the main clause.

1 If I __became__ (become) an astronaut, I __could go__ (go) to the moon. (possible outcome)

2 If I _____ (meet) the president, I _____ (not know) what to say. (predicted result)

3 I _____ (become) an astronaut if I _____ (study) astrophysics. (possible outcome)

4 If I _____ (be) more patient, I _____ (get) a Ph.D. in physics. (predicted result)

5 If I _____ (not be) busy next week, I _____ (go) to the meeting. (predicted result)

6 Robyn _____ (think) of good solutions if she _____ (understand) the issue. (possible outcome)

7 The program _____ (be) more likely to succeed if the government _____ (give) more money. (predicted result)

8 If more interesting things _____ (happen), more people _____ (be) willing to give money to the project. (predicted result)

5 Complete the predictions about the future with your own ideas.

1 If NASA sends people to Mars in the 2030s, _____
_____ .

2 If more people studied astrophysics and astronomy, _____
_____ .

3 If space travel were as easy as traveling on a plane, _____
_____ .

4 If the government stopped paying for space exploration, _____
_____ .

6 Work with a partner. Say your sentences from Exercise 5 aloud. Were your predictions similar or different? Which do you think are more likely to happen?

PREPARING TO LISTEN

UNDERSTANDING
KEY VOCABULARY

PRISM Online Workbook

1 You are going to listen to a discussion about the ways to pay for space exploration. Read the sentences. Choose the best definition for the words in bold.

1 We have two **options** for exploring Mars – we can send robots, or we can send people.
   a choices
   b opinions

2 The American space program NASA has a **public** part of their website where anyone in the world can see their projects and give ideas for how to use some of their inventions.
   a only for one person or group and not for everyone
   b open to everyone to see or use

3 **Private** companies want to do research in space exploration. They do not receive money from the government, and they pay for the research themselves.
   a controlled by a person or a company and not the government
   b controlled by the government

4 An astronomer is an **expert** in the study of space. He or she often has a Ph.D. or a very advanced degree in the field.
   a someone who does not know a lot about something
   b someone who has a lot of knowledge about something or a lot of skill in something

5 The company hired a recent college graduate who had a lot of **talent**. The company was very happy that its new employee could do the job so well.
   a a natural ability to do something
   b good grades

6 The supervisor **evaluated** the project to see if it was good enough for the company to continue to spend money on it.
   a fixed something
   b considered or studied something carefully and decided how good or bad it was

2 Work with a partner. Look at the photo and answer the questions.

1 Do photos like these make you feel interested in learning more about space exploration? Why?

2 Who do you think pays for exploring space?

WHILE LISTENING

3 ▶ 8.5 Listen to the first part of the talk introducing the discussion. Complete the sentences from the introduction.

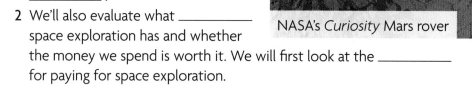

1 We'll begin today's discussion with a look at how to pay for space _____ .

2 We'll also evaluate what _____ space exploration has and whether

NASA's *Curiosity* Mars rover

the money we spend is worth it. We will first look at the _____ for paying for space exploration.

4 You are going to listen to the second part of the discussion. What do you think the purpose of the discussion will be? Choose the most likely option.

1 to describe what space exploration is like

2 to think about options for paying for space exploration and the good and bad points of exploring space

3 to make a new plan for future space exploration and for humans living on other planets

5 Work with a partner. Predict the topics that will be included in the discussion.

1 time taken to travel to other parts of space

2 the benefits of space exploration

3 space exploration projects being done now

4 money spent on space exploration

5 the number of people working in space exploration

6 who pays for space explorers

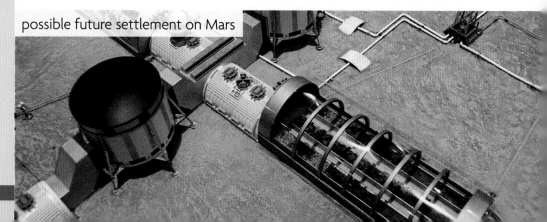

possible future settlement on Mars

6 ▶ 8.6 Listen to the second part of the discussion. Listen for each speaker's opinions and reasons. Complete the student's notes.

speaker	opinion	reason
Dr. Chen Wu	Wants funding from (1)_____	Space exploration is (2)_____ Space explorations shows us how (3)_____, what stars do, the effects on people
Raj Padow	Wants funding from (4)_____	Because companies get (5)_____ from discoveries made in space exploration
Dorota Loy	Wants funding from (6)_____ places	Because (7)_____ benefits from space exploration Get funding from governments, private companies, and (8)_____ people giving money on (9)_____

7 ▶ 8.6 Listen again. Use your notes to check your answers to Exercises 4 and 5.

DISCUSSION

8 Use your notes from Listening 1 and Listening 2 to discuss the following questions in small groups.

1 Do you think people should try to go to Mars? Why?
2 Who do you think should pay for space exploration? Why?

9 Look at the picture and discuss the questions with a partner. Use your notes to support your answers.

1 Do you think people will live on Mars in the future?
2 What would be the benefits for people?
3 Would there be any disadvantages?
4 Would you like to visit or live there? Why?
5 If you lived there, what would you do in your free time?

SPEAKING

CRITICAL THINKING

At the end of this unit, you are going to do the Speaking Task below.

> Discuss how to get children interested in space exploration.

 REMEMBER

1 Look back at your notes from Listening 2 with a partner. What is the main problem that the speakers discuss? Write your answer in the "problem" column of the table.

problem	possible solution 1
	possible solution 2
	possible solution 3
	possible solution 4

2 What solutions did the speakers suggest? Add them to the "possible solution" spaces in the table.

APPLY

3 Discuss in pairs the kinds of problems that can happen when you try to get people interested in an issue. Write notes about the topics.

1 level of interest

a _____

b _____

2 getting children involved

a _____

b _____

3 children coming regularly

a _____

b _____

4 Choose one of the problems about getting children interested in space exploration. Write the problem and possible solutions in the table. You will use this information in the Speaking Task at the end of this unit.

ANALYZE

1 Children these days don't think space is interesting because there isn't anything exciting happening. So they might not want to come to an astronomy club.

2 We are in a city, and in cities it is hard to see the stars.

3 Children these days want fast-moving entertainment, like video games and television, so they might get bored.

4 Equipment like telescopes are expensive, and we don't have much money.

5 Our club is in a small town far away from astronomy experts, like college professors. How can we find an expert to help us?

problem	possible solution 1
	possible solution 2
	possible solution 3
	possible solution 4

5 Work in small groups. Take turns sharing your answers for the problem you chose. Did your group choose the same or different solutions?

6 Discuss the questions about problem solving in small groups.

EVALUATE

1 Can you think of any other ways to organize your ideas about problems and solutions? Look back at the different tables in the units of the book to help you.

2 What kind of information can you give to support your ideas for possible solutions? Think of supporting ideas you can add to the table in Exercise 4 to help you.

TURN-TAKING

1 People often use fixed phrases to invite others to speak, interrupt, or continue speaking when someone has stopped them. Write the phrases in the correct column in the table.

> **a** What is your opinion?
> **b** Can I finish?
> **c** I'd like to finish my point.
> **d** Can I just say something?
> **e** Sorry, but I have to interrupt you and say …
> **f** You haven't said much. What do you think?
> **g** Why don't you start us off … ?
> **h** Sorry, but can I just say … ?
> **i** Would anybody like to say anything else about … ?
> **j** Let me just finish what I was saying.

inviting someone else to speak	interrupting	continuing to speak
Let's get your thoughts on this.	Can I just say something here?	Can I finish my point? Please allow me to finish.

2 Write the phrases from Exercise 1 to complete the dialogue. In some items, more than one answer is possible.

Halil: We are discussing the best way to travel when going on vacation. (1)_____ Ramona?

Ramona: For me, it is definitely the train. You can relax and watch the world go by as you travel, and –

Shin: (2)_____ ? Doesn't that depend on the train? In many cities, you can't sit down. Trains are too crowded and –

Ramona: (3)_____ . You can relax and watch the world go by, but that's in a city where the trains are not too busy.

Halil: (4)_____ trains?

Lisa: No, but I'd like to talk about bikes. They are the cheapest way to travel.

Ramona: I agree. It is another good way to travel.

Halil: And Roberto, (5)_____ ? (6)_____ ?

Roberto: Sorry! I wasn't listening!

3 Work in small groups. Read the dialogue aloud.

4 Divide the phrases into those we use to start a discussion and those we use to finish a discussion. Write *S* (start) or *F* (finish).

1 Let me begin by asking ... _____

2 Let me end this by saying ... _____

3 We'll begin today's discussion by ... _____

4 Would you like to start? _____

5 So, to conclude ... _____

6 Finally, ... _____

SHOWING LEVELS OF AGREEMENT

SKILLS

In discussions it is important to let others know that you understand their points and how much you agree with them. You can show you agree with someone by using these phrases:

Phrases showing strong agreement:

I agree with you completely / 100 percent.

You're absolutely right.

I feel exactly the same.

That's a good point.

You can let others know that you have understood their points, even if you don't agree with them, by using these phrases:

Phrases showing weak agreement or understanding (but maybe not agreeing):

I suppose / guess so.

You could / might be right.

You have a point.

I see your point.

I hear what you're saying, (but) ...

5 Choose a phrase from the box to complete the dialogue. Use the words in parentheses to help you choose phrases for strong or weak agreement. In some items, more than one answer is possible.

Ela: I think that it is really important for children to have an interest in space exploration – we need to make sure these important programs continue into the future.

Carlos: I (1)_____ (weak). But do you think we really need a lot of kids interested in space?

Hao: Hmm. Carlos, (2)_____ , (weak) but Ela has a good point. Even if people don't work on space exploration, we still need engineers so we have satellites orbit for our phones and GPS.

Ela: (3)_____ , (strong) Hao. And we have satellites for predicting the weather, too.

Carlos: (4)_____ . (strong) I don't want to lose those things. But I don't think kids need to get interested in living on Mars.

Ela: Hmm. (5)_____ (weak) Well, who knows what will happen with global warming and our future. Don't you think it would be good to have some options?

Hao: I think both of you (6)_____ (weak). Still, maybe it is good to at least be sure children know about space exploration.

SPEAKING TASK

Discuss how to get children interested in space exploration.

PREPARE

1 Look back at your notes from Critical Thinking. Add any new information to the table.

2 Work in small groups. Share your ideas for how you can get children interested in space exploration. Follow these steps.

- Use the table in Exercise 4 in Critical Thinking as an example to help you.
- Make sure that you discuss possible problems and solutions.
- Use the language in Preparation for Speaking to take turns in your discussion, to show different levels of agreement, and to acknowledge other people's ideas.

3 You are going to discuss your ideas with another group. Choose which points from your discussion in Exercise 2 you will discuss.

4 Refer to the Task Checklist below as you prepare for your discussion.

TASK CHECKLIST	✔
Use phrases to acknowledge and agree with others' points.	
Discuss possible problems and solutions.	
Use future unreal conditionals accurately.	
Use phrases for turn-taking and for starting and finishing a discussion.	

DISCUSS

5 Work with another group. Take turns discussing your ideas. Take notes on the other group's ideas and any problems you see for their plan. Ask follow-up questions.

6 In the same group, decide which ideas are best.

7 Compare your final plan with other groups. Which is the best plan?

REVIEWING FOR EXAMS

PREPARING TO LISTEN

1 Work in small groups and discuss the questions.

1 How often do you take tests or exams?
2 What kinds of tests or exams have you taken?
3 When was the last time that you took an exam?
4 How do you usually review for tests and exams?

WHILE LISTENING

2 ▶ 8.7 Listen to Sergio, Li Chao, and Anna describe how they prepare for exams. Circle the strategies that you hear.

> organizing notes   practicing test questions   making an idea map
> joining a study group   studying with a friend

3 ▶ 8.7 Complete the table below with the strategy used by each student. Then listen again and write the reason why each student uses that particular strategy.

Name	Strategy	Reason
Sergio		
Li Chao		
Anna		

4 Work with a partner and compare your answers.

Exam review strategies

Next time you have a test or exam, think about what review strategies you could use to help you. Not everyone prefers the same strategies – find out what works for you!

PRACTICE

5 Read the list of review strategies. Match each strategy with a reason.

1 Organize and reread all of your notes from class. _____
2 Read chapter summaries or review sheets that your teacher has prepared. _____
3 Teach the material to a friend, or form a study group. _____
4 If possible, study past test papers and sample answers. _____
5 Review the course material regularly during the semester. _____

a You won't have to study everything the night before.
b It's important to know what kinds of questions to expect.
c Teachers often emphasize the most important points during class.
d Helping other people understand the material can help you understand it better.
e This can help you identify main ideas that will be covered on the test.

6 Work in small groups. Discuss the questions.

1 Have you used any of these strategies? Which ones?
2 What other strategies do you know or use for reviewing material?

REAL-WORLD APPLICATION

7 Imagine you are going to create a test on what you have studied in Unit 8. Answer the questions.

1 What will you put in the test? (Grammar? Vocabulary? Listening? Speaking?)
2 How many parts will the test have?
3 How many points will you give for each part?
4 How should your classmates prepare for the test?

8 Work with a partner and compare your plans. Did you include the same things?

UNIT 5
ROLE CARD STUDENT A

You are the parent of someone who wants to become a professional athlete. What do you think about the money spent on athletes? Why? Use the persuasive map on page 117 to help you.

ROLE CARD STUDENT B

You are a charity worker. Your charity helps poor people get food and medicine. What do you think about the money spent on athletes? Why? Use the persuasive map on page 117 to help you.

ROLE CARD STUDENT C

You are a journalist, and you write about sports for the newspaper. What do you think about the money spent on athletes? Why? Use the persuasive map on page 117 to help you.

ROLE CARD STUDENT D

You are a famous soccer star. What do you think about the money spent on athletes? Why? Use the persuasive map on page 117 to help you.

UNIT 6
STUDENT A

1 Tell student B your problems. Use the ideas below. Then listen to student B's advice.

   1 Everyone is late for meetings and wastes my time.
   2 When I have to speak English in the meeting, I get too nervous to speak.
   3 I can't use the computer very well.

2 Listen to student B's problems. Give him or her some advice.

UNIT 6
STUDENT B

1 Listen to student A's problems. Give him or her some advice.

2 Tell student A your problems. Use the ideas below. Then listen to student A's advice.

   1 People leave the meeting room very messy after meetings, and you have to clean it up.
   2 You keep forgetting meetings and appointments.
   3 You find it difficult to do presentations because you get too nervous.

GLOSSARY OF KEY VOCABULARY

Words that are part of the Academic Word List are noted with an (A) in this glossary.

UNIT 1 PLACES

LISTENING 1

ancient (adj) from a long time ago; very old

apartment (n) a room or set of rooms in a building for someone to live in

bridge (n) something built over a river or road that lets people, cars, or trains go across

capital (n) the most important city in a country or state, where the government is

cave (n) a large hole in the side of a mountain or under the ground

recognize (v) to know something because you have seen it before

rock (n) a hard piece of material that the Earth is made of

strange (adj) different from the usual or normal; unusual or not expected

LISTENING 2

area (A) (n) a part of a larger place

field (n) open, grassy land

lake (n) a body of water that has land all around it

located (A) (adj) in a certain place

modern (adj) relating to the present time and not to the past

traffic (n) all the cars and trucks using the road

urban (adj) belonging to or related to a city

woods (n) a place with a lot of trees growing near each other

UNIT 2 FESTIVALS AND CELEBRATIONS

LISTENING 1

activity (n) something you do for fun

band (n) a group of musicians who play music together

culture (A) (n) the habits and traditions of a country or group of people

enjoy (v) to get pleasure from

entertainment (n) shows, movies, games, or other ways of having fun

lecture (A) (n) a formal talk given to a group of people to teach them about a subject

traditional (A) (adj) part of older ways of doing things and older ideas that are not modern

LISTENING 2

celebrate (v) to do something fun because it is a special day or because something good has happened

costume (n) clothes that people wear to make them look like someone or something else

decorate (v) to make something look pretty by putting things on it

dish (n) one type of food prepared as part of a bigger meal

fireworks (n) small objects that explode to make a loud noise and bright colors, and are often used for special events

gift (n) something special that you give to someone else

parade (n) a line of people or vehicles that moves through the street to celebrate a special day or event

UNIT 3 THE INTERNET AND TECHNOLOGY

LISTENING 1

accident (n) something bad that happens that is not on purpose and that causes injury or damage

collect (v) to get things from different places and bring them together

develop (v) to make something new

disabled (adj) having an illness or injury that makes it difficult to do things that other people do

information (n) facts about a situation, person, event, etc.

luxury (n) something expensive that you enjoy but do not need

robot (n) a machine controlled by a computer that can move and do other things that people can do

suit (n) an outfit of a jacket and pants or a jacket and skirt that are made from the same material

LISTENING 2

difficult (adj) not easy; needing skill or effort to do or understand

file Ⓐ (n) a collection of information stored in one place on a computer

location Ⓐ (n) a place where something is found

memory (n) your ability to remember

research Ⓐ (n) detailed study of a subject to learn more about it

stupid (adj) silly or not intelligent

UNIT 4 WEATHER AND CLIMATE

LISTENING 1

angry (adj) having a strong feeling against someone who has behaved badly, making you want to shout at them or hurt them; mad

cool (adj) slightly cold; of a low temperature

dry (adj) without water or liquid in, on, or around something

energy Ⓐ (n) the power and ability to do something or be active

humid (adj) having a lot of moisture in the air

prefer (v) to choose or want one thing instead of another

upset (adj) unhappy or worried because something unpleasant has happened

LISTENING 2

become (v) to begin to be something

believe (v) to think that something is true and correct

carefully (adv) with great attention

discover (v) to find something for the first time

disappear (v) to stop existing in the world

take care of (phr v) to care for or be responsible for someone or something

save (v) to bring something back to good condition; to keep something from harm

unusual (adj) different from what is common or expected

UNIT 5 SPORTS AND COMPETITION

LISTENING 1

champion (n) someone who wins a competition

compete (v) to do an activity with others and try to do it better than they do

hit (v) to touch something quickly and forcefully with the hand or an object

intelligent Ⓐ (adj) able to understand and learn well

kick (v) to hit someone or something with the foot

strong (adj) physically powerful

LISTENING 2

charge (v) to ask someone to pay for something, especially for an activity or a service

competition (n) an organized event in which people try to win by being the best, the fastest, etc.

cost (n) the amount of money that you need to buy or do something

fan (n) someone who likes a famous person, sport, type of music, etc.

prize (n) something valuable that is given to someone who wins a game or has done good work

salary (n) the amount of money that you get from your job, usually every two weeks or every month

score (v) to get points in a game or on a test

support (v) to take care of someone by paying for his or her food, clothes, etc.

UNIT 6 BUSINESS

LISTENING 1

break (n) a stop in an activity for a short time

colleague Ⓐ (n) someone who works with you

earn (v) to get money from doing work

profit (n) money that you make from selling goods or services for more than they cost to make or provide

project Ⓐ (n) a piece of work that is for a particular purpose or a detailed study of a topic

spend time (v phr) to use time to do something

waste time (v phr) to use time badly

LISTENING 2

careless (adj) done, made, or said without paying attention

customer (n) someone who buys goods or services from a business

goal Ⓐ (n) something you want to do successfully in the future

messy (adj) untidy or dirty

skill (n) the ability to do an activity or job well

strength (n) a good quality or ability that makes someone good at something

stress Ⓐ (n) feelings of worry caused by problems

weakness (n) a quality of someone or something that is not good

UNIT 7 PEOPLE

LISTENING 1

achievement Ⓐ (n) something good and successful that you do, usually by working hard

complicated (adj) having a lot of different pieces, in a way that is difficult to understand

design Ⓐ (n) the way something is planned and made

invention (n) something made for the first time

point (n) an opinion, fact, or idea that is said or written

purpose (n) why you do something or why something is present

simple (adj) not difficult or complicated; without extra things that are not needed

use (n) a reason why something is used

LISTENING 2

amazing (adj) very surprising

entrepreneur (n) someone who starts his or her own business

remarkable (adj) very unusual or noticeable in a way that you admire

retire (v) to leave your job and stop working, usually because you get older

situation (n) the things that are happening and are present at a particular time and place

success (n) something that has a good result

UNIT 8 THE UNIVERSE

LISTENING 1

beyond (prep) on the other side of something

explore (v) to travel around a place to find out what is there

journey (n) a long trip from one place to another

path (n) the direction that a person or thing moves in

planet (n) a large, round object in space that moves around the sun or another star

reach (v) to arrive somewhere

spacecraft (n) a vehicle that can travel into space

surface (n) the top or outside part of something

LISTENING 2

evaluate Ⓐ (v) to consider or study something carefully and decide how good or bad it is

expert Ⓐ (n) someone who has a lot of knowledge about something or a lot of skill in something

option Ⓐ (n) a choice

private (adj) controlled by a person or a company and not the government

public (adj) open to everyone to see or use

talent (n) a natural ability to do something

UNIT 1

▶ **The Grand Canal**

This is Venice, Italy. It is full of fantastic palaces and beautiful churches, and, of course, a lot of canals.

There are 117 little islands between the canals, and 400 bridges. Historically, Venice is an important city for art and business. But these days, most people know it as a popular tourist center.

The Grand Canal is the largest canal in Venice. It's more than two miles long. It's Venice's busiest road, but you won't see cars here. Instead, you'll see a kind of boat called the gondola.

At one time, there was probably a river here, but the Grand Canal is man-made. The palaces and other buildings are on stilts – long legs – that go deep into the ground under the canal.

A gondola ride takes about half an hour. It's one of the best 30 minutes you can spend in your life.

Here is the Ca' d'Oro, one of Venice's most beautiful palaces. It was built in the 15th century and was then decorated with gold.

And this is the Rialto Bridge, the oldest bridge across the Grand Canal. It's made of stone, and for nearly 300 years, it was the only way to cross the Grand Canal on foot. No wonder two of Venice's nicknames are "The City of Bridges" and "The Bride of the Sea."

🔊 **1.1**

place	quick
hot	up

🔊 **1.2**

James: Welcome to the Travel Podcast. I'm James. I'm here with Suzie, and today we're looking at unusual places where people actually live. Suzie, when you traveled, did you see any interesting or **strange** homes around the world?

Suzie: Well, it depends what you mean by strange. I live in a single-family house, so the **apartment** buildings in New York, for example, seem pretty strange to me.

James: I really mean places that very few people know about …

Suzie: Oh, I see … Umm. Well, when I was on vacation last year in Arizona, I saw some tall apartment buildings made out of mud. You could say they are interesting.

James: Yes, they are very interesting! And so are the cave houses at a place called Matmata.

Suzie: Matmata? Is that in Egypt?

James: No, it's in Tunisia. Take a look at the picture. You might **recognize** it from the *Star Wars* films. They filmed some of the scenes there because the cave houses look strange, like maybe they aren't real. But actually, these houses in the **caves** are real. People started living in them 700 years ago. They made them out of the **rock**.

Suzie: Wow! That's **ancient**! Where is it exactly?

James: It's about 220 miles, so around 355 kilometers, south of the **capital**, Tunis. I'd love to go there. Actually, when I was younger I went to Cappadocia in Turkey. It was fantastic! There are cave houses there, too. It's in Anatolia in the center of Turkey. Take a look.

Suzie: The buildings look like mushrooms!

James: Interesting place, isn't it? The caves formed from rock more than 8,000 years ago. People changed them into homes during the Roman period. Some people still live there now.

Suzie: Now? That's amazing. But did you know that some people live on **bridges**? Look at these two pictures.

James: Oh yeah. This one is beautiful, and it looks very old. It's in Italy isn't it? Is it Rome?

Suzie: Well, it is in Italy. It's called the Ponte Vecchio, but it's actually in Florence, north of Rome. They built the bridge in 1345. There was another bridge there before, but an accident destroyed it. So they made this one, and people started to live there. It's amazing, isn't it?

James: Yes, it is. But the bridge in the other picture looks newer.

Suzie: Yeah that's Neft Dashlari in Azerbaijan.

James: Where?

Suzie: Azerbaijan. You know — A-Z-E-R-B-A-I-J-A-N.

James: Oh, OK. It looks really long, and it looks like it has a lot of factories. Do a lot of people work there?

Suzie: Yes, they drill for oil from under the sea there. They decided that the workers needed somewhere to live, so they built a kind of "city" above the sea. The bridge is 30 miles long. That's about 48 kilometers. They put houses, libraries, schools, and even a movie theater there.

James: Really? So, hundreds of people live there?

Suzie: About 2,000 people live there. It even appeared in a *James Bond* movie.

James: Well, it makes my house look really boring!

Suzie: Mine, too!

 1.3

Teacher: OK, everyone. Today we are talking about interesting places.

I'd like to talk about the city of Vancouver, in British Columbia, Canada. It's one of the most beautiful cities in the world. We often think cities are **urban areas**, with **traffic** and **modern** buildings. We do not usually think cities have **woods**, **lakes**, and **fields**. But Vancouver is a "green city" — a place that is good to live in because it has clean air, water, and land. Vancouver has the best parts of green forests and city life. I would like to talk about some history of Vancouver as well as some of the advantages and disadvantages of this "green" city.

Vancouver originally was a place where the native people of the area lived and traded for thousands of years before Europeans came to live there in the 1800s. Then in 1886, at the first city meeting, the people of Vancouver asked the national government to give the city 1,000 acres to use as a park. They got the land from the government and started Stanley Park. This was the start of Vancouver becoming a green city with many parks and beautiful views. But being a green city with lots of parks has both advantages and disadvantages.

First of all, let's look at some of the advantages. Obviously, Stanley Park is a large park. In fact, because it is **located** in the city of Vancouver, it is the third largest urban park in North America. It has many gardens, walking paths, trees, and even animals, like bald eagles, coyotes, and seals. As we know, lots of trees help clean the city air. Also, lots of parks give people many places to walk, so they are healthier. Since Vancouver is near the mountains and the ocean, people can enjoy the outdoors easily during the warm, sunny summers. When people go to Stanley Park, they can enjoy ancient trees as they walk near the ocean, or they can have fun by Beaver

Lake, which, like Stanley Park, helps make Vancouver one of the healthiest and cleanest cities in the world.

I'd also like to talk about some disadvantages of Stanley Park and Vancouver. Space in a city is very important. Having many parks means that people have less space to build houses and apartments. Because Vancouver is located between the mountains and the ocean, there is not much room for new buildings. This makes Vancouver an expensive city. Also, when you have a beautiful place to live, a lot of people want to go there. This makes the city crowded. Actually, Vancouver has very bad traffic. Lastly, when you have a lot of parks, wild animals in the parks can sometimes be a problem. For example, Stanley Park gives information to people about what to do if they see a coyote. In my opinion, having coyotes in a city park is bad.

Finally, while I think these disadvantages might mean that some people would not want to visit Vancouver, I personally feel that most people would enjoy Vancouver. In my opinion, being close to nature and having a healthy city are worth paying a little more money. And a lot of people agree with this idea because Vancouver is a very popular place to visit and live. So I will recommend that people visit Vancouver and enjoy the many parks; the clean, healthy city; and the interesting sights.

🔊 1.4

1 Obviously, Stanley Park is a large park.
2 In fact, because it is located in the city of Vancouver, it is the third largest urban park in North America.
3 As we know, lots of trees help clean the city air.
4 Finally, while I think these disadvantages might mean that some people would not want to visit Vancouver, ...
5 ... I personally feel that most people would enjoy Vancouver.

6 In my opinion, being close to nature and having a healthy city are worth paying a little more money.

🔊 1.5

1 I'd like to talk about the city of Vancouver, in British Columbia, Canada.
2 First of all, let's look at some of the advantages.
3 I'd also like to talk about some disadvantages of Stanley Park and Vancouver.
4 Finally, while I think these disadvantages mean that some people would not want to visit Vancouver, I personally feel that most people would enjoy Vancouver.

🔊 1.6

I'd like to talk about the city of Vancouver, in British Columbia, Canada.

🔊 1.7

First of all, let's look at some of the advantages.

🔊 1.8

Hi, everyone! Our tour today begins right here, at the Administration Building. This is where you come to pay your tuition, or get information about the university.

This is University Square. It's my favorite place on campus. It's a great place to take a break or meet your friends. In the summer there are always a lot of people here, sitting in the sun.

Now we are in front of the Smith Library. The library is open 24 hours a day, 7 days a week. It's very popular of course, especially during final exams. We have study areas here for students working with a study group, but there are also silent areas if you prefer to study alone. We have more than 100 computers here for students to use, and printers too, of course.

This building is the Student Union. As you can see, there's the bookstore, where you can buy the books you need for your classes. There's a cafeteria on the ground floor, where you can get lunch or a snack.

This building next to the Student Union is the Career Center. Here you can find out about jobs on campus. They can help you prepare for interviews as well.

OK, our last stop is the Browning Gym. You can get in here for free with your student ID card. There's a pool, a couple of basketball courts, and lots of exercise machines. They also have classes in yoga and dance.

UNIT 2

▶ Harbin's Ice Festival

Seth Doane (reporter): There's no thaw here, at least that's what organizers are hoping. Harbin is called "the Ice City," and for good reason. Every year for 30 years now, it's hosted an ice festival, making the most of its bitter Siberian temperatures by building a mini-city out of ice. It's minus 11 Fahrenheit today, which is about average, but that does not stop visitors. More than a million people are expected to turn out to see the spectacle.

Kristen Ing: It's absolutely amazing.

Seth Doane: Kristen Ing and Alex Clark are two of them. 7,000 people worked to put this together, using enough ice and snow to fill nearly 200 Boeing 747 cargo planes. There are ice slides, ice temples, and even an ice Empire State Building. If you tire from seeing too much of it, Mom can just drag you home. Every year this ice festival begins on January 5. The end date is not so certain. That depends on the temperature. Ultimately, everything here will just melt away. For CBS This Morning Saturday, Seth Doane, Harbin, China.

🔊 **2.1**

Reporter: Today I'm at the Festival of Ideas, which has been held in the U.K. each October since 2008. It's a free festival with lots of activities organized by the University of Cambridge. But it isn't just for students. Anyone interested in art and science can go to the **lectures**, talks, classes, and performances. The festival gets bigger and bigger every year; the first year, 7,000 people attended, but by the third year that number had almost doubled. We asked one of the visitors about the festival.

Reporter: Hello, there. Can you introduce yourself and tell me, is this your first time at the festival here in Cambridge?

Judith: My name is Judith. And no, I come here every year!

Reporter: Can you tell us about why you like coming to the festival?

Judith: Well, it's an interesting event to come to. It's great for kids and adults. I **enjoy** learning about all the new ideas people have on important topics. We don't get much time to really think or learn about new things in everyday life, but you can do exactly that at this festival.

Reporter: So, what kinds of things do people learn? Do people concentrate on learning just one thing?

Judith: No, most people plan on going to several events. For example, today I studied some history. I just went to a lecture about the English Civil War, which happened from 1642 to 1651. It was really interesting! The day before, I played games to find out about gravity. It was a science **activity**. And tomorrow, I'm going to a lecture on the global economy, which I'm sure will really make me think!

Reporter: Are there any things you don't like about it? Are you ever bored?

Judith: Not really. The only problem is that it's really crowded!

Reporter: Judith, like many others, is really enjoying the Festival of Ideas. Nowadays around the world, there are more and more new festivals, often based on music, food, or **culture**. Take Iceland Airwaves for example … Iceland Airwaves is another festival held in October. In 1999, organizers started holding this festival every year in Reykjavik, the capital of Iceland. Isak works at the festival. Hi, Isak.

Isak: Hi. Welcome to Iceland Airwaves!

Reporter: Thanks. So, what happens here?

Isak: Well, as you can hear, it's a music festival. We have many **bands** from all over the world, and we try to present new and interesting music.

Reporter: Do you have many people here from other countries?

Isak: Yes. Our visitors are from all over the world. In addition to the music, there are lots of clubs, and people can go sightseeing, too. There are some beautiful, natural places. Some people prefer to visit Reykjavik's many museums. I think it's the best music festival around now!

Reporter: Well, I hope you enjoy the rest of the event! Visiting such festivals is not just for **entertainment**; it's also a fantastic way to find out about the culture of a different country. Nasrra is visiting the Muscat Festival with her family. This is held in January and February each year in Oman, and Nasrra has been coming for the last couple of years. Hi, Nasrra. Are you enjoying the festival?

Nasrra: Yeah! It's wonderful!

Reporter: Can you tell us something about the festival?

Nasrra: Of course. It's a chance for people to learn about the heritage and culture of Oman.

Reporter: So, why are you here?

Nasrra: My mother and father want to watch some of the sports; there was cycling last year and also a camel race. You can also learn **traditional** dance. But I decided to go to the fashion show.

Reporter: That sounds great.

Nasrra: Yeah. And after we finish watching the races and shows, we'll go and eat some traditional food.

Reporter: So these international festivals, with lots of music, food, dance, and fashion, are providing a different type of experience for people.

🔊 **2.2**

Well, it's an interesting event to come to.

🔊 **2.3**

1 So, what kinds of things do people learn?
2 Are there any things you don't like about it?
3 Do you have many people here from other countries?

🔊 **2.4**

Lisa: Paul, what's your opinion? Which is the best North American holiday or celebration?

Paul: Hmm. Well, I like Independence Day in the U.S. because of the **fireworks**, and New Year's Eve often has fireworks, too. And Valentine's Day has **gifts**, like chocolates. But I think the best holiday is Thanksgiving.

Lisa: Why do you like Thanksgiving?

Paul: We all have something to be thankful for, so everyone can **celebrate** it. Both the U.S. and Canada celebrate it.

Lisa: Really? How do people celebrate it?

Paul: Well, most people get together with family and friends and have a big meal.

Lisa: What do they eat?

Paul: They usually eat a traditional meal. This is usually a delicious turkey with stuffing for the main **dish**. You should try it. Most traditional Thanksgiving meals have food that is from the Americas, like potatoes, corn, and cranberries.

For dessert, we eat pumpkin pie, but some people prefer different kinds of pie, like apple.

Lisa: Is the food the same in both countries?

Paul: Actually, there are some differences in the food. In Canada, for example, the pumpkin pie is spicy, but in the U.S. it's sweet. I like the American style, with whipped cream. You have to try it. Another dish that is different is the stuffing. For instance, in Canada stuffing is often made from rice or bread, but in the southern U.S. it could be made from cornbread. In the eastern U.S., sometimes oysters are used in the stuffing.

Lisa: That all sounds delicious. Are there any special decorations for Thanksgiving?

Paul: Well, people often **decorate** their dinner tables and homes with things such as colorful leaves, fall vegetables, and candles. The decorations usually have fall colors, like red, yellow, and orange.

Lisa: Do people give gifts or do some special activities?

Paul: Yeah, there are some special activities. For example, both countries celebrate with **parades** with marching bands and people in **costumes**. It's also traditional to watch sports on TV. But people don't give gifts for Thanksgiving.

Lisa: It sounds like the celebration is almost the same in both countries.

Paul: Well, there are some differences between Canadian and American Thanksgiving.

Lisa: Like what?

Paul: In Canada, for instance, the holiday is celebrated on the second Monday in October. But in the U.S. it's on the fourth Thursday in November. Another difference is that in Canada people enjoy small, local parades. In the U.S. they have a huge parade in New York City, and people all over the U.S. watch it on TV.

People in the New York parade sometimes wear costumes. One last difference is that each country has different reasons for the holiday. In Canada the holiday celebrates the fall harvest. But Americans celebrate the fall harvest and remembering the Native Americans helping settlers hunt and grow food.

Lisa: That sounds like a lot of fun. I want to go to a Thanksgiving celebration in both countries!

🔊 **2.5**

1 ... some people prefer different kinds of pie, like apple.

2 ... people often decorate their dinner tables and homes with things such as colorful leaves, fall vegetables, and candles.

3 For example, both countries celebrate with parades with marching bands and people in costumes.

4 In Canada, for instance, the holiday is celebrated on the second Monday in October.

🔊 **2.6**

Conversation 1

Adam: Hi. I'm Adam.

Cindy: Hi. I'm Cindy.

Adam: Nice to meet you.

Cindy: Yeah.

Adam: Where are you from?

Cindy: I'm from Korea.

Adam: Really? Wow. How long have you been in the U.S.?

Cindy: About a year ... What about you? Where are you from?

Adam: I'm from Chicago.

Cindy: That's a big city.

Adam: Yeah! It's very different from here.

Cindy: Really? How is it different?

Adam: It's colder in the winter. I like the weather here.

Cindy: Me too. In my city it's really humid in the summer, and I hate that.

Adam: What city are you from?

Cindy: Busan. It's in the south of Korea.

Adam: Oh.

Cindy: What's your major?

Adam: I'm not sure yet. Maybe business management.

Cindy: Oh, me too! What classes are you in?

Conversation 2

Joe: Your English is very good. How long have you been here?

Ahmad: I've been in the U.S. for three years. But this is my first year here.

Joe: How do you like it so far?

Ahmad: It's good. I like the campus a lot.

Joe: Yeah, me too.

Ahmad: Do you live on campus?

Joe: Yeah ... Do you?

Ahmad: No. Actually I have an apartment off campus.

Joe: Oh! What's that like?

Ahmad: It's great. I live with two friends. But it's pretty far. It takes about forty minutes to get to school.

Joe: Really? You take the bus?

Ahmad: Yeah ... And the other problem is, it's harder to meet people. My roommates both speak Arabic, so we don't practice English very much.

Joe: Do you play a sport?

Ahmad: Not right now. But I play soccer at home.

Joe: Oh! Well, if you like to play soccer, there's a group of us that play a couple of times a week – just for fun. Would you like to come along?

Ahmad: Oh, that sounds good. Yeah. I'm interested.

Joe: OK. Well, give me your phone number and ...

UNIT 3

▶ Fiber Optic Cables

In the middle of the ocean, deep underwater, violent volcanic activity changes the ocean floor.

Usually we don't know anything about this – until the Internet stops working.

99% of all Internet traffic between continents goes through cables at the bottom of the ocean.

But sometimes there are problems. For example, 10 years ago nine important fiber optic cables on the ocean floor between Taiwan and the Philippines suddenly went dead.

Computers all over Asia crashed. Engineers looked for the problem, and they found that the cables were broken.

Volcanic activity caused heavy rocks to move and break the cables.

Suddenly, many people in Southeast Asia couldn't use the Internet. What would happen to businesses? It took weeks to find and repair the cables.

Engineers used this special ship, called the Wave Sentinel. Its job is to keep the Internet connected.

🔊 3.1

disabled	save
fish	shave
kitchen	watch
suit	wash
pollution	

🔊 3.2

1 station		**7** match	
2 sort		**8** ocean	
3 short		**9** accident	
4 wish		**10** cheap	
5 which			
6 robots			

🔊 **3.3**

1 sorts
2 cheap
3 wash
4 sea
5 shave

🔊 **3.4**

Host: Welcome to University Radio, the station run by students for students. I'm Chen Hu, and this is Science Today. Our subject is technological development, and our guest is Professor James Holden, expert in robotics. Thanks for coming in, Professor. When we think of **robots**, we generally think of science fiction movies. Is this out of date?

Professor: Yes, it is. Technology has **developed** very fast over the last ten years, and robots are part of everyday life. Robots can now do many important things.

Host: What kinds of things?

Professor: Well, they have been used in factories for years; Japan and China have the most industrial robots in the world. But now robots are coming into our lives in other ways. In Japan, Thailand, and Hong Kong, for example, there are robot waiters in restaurants, and in South Korea a robot is used as an English teacher. Robots weren't used very much in the past, since they were always really expensive. But because they have become cheaper, they are being used in new and interesting ways. Another key area is the way robots can help with medical care.

Host: Can you explain that a little more?

Professor: Well, a good example is the robotic **suit** for **disabled** people. Robots can now assist people who can't walk. They can help them to move again. People "wear" the robot, like clothes. The robot then helps move the person's arms or legs. For example, one man, Joey Abbica, couldn't walk because of an **accident** at work three years earlier. Before the accident, Joey could surf really well. In fact, he won lots of competitions, but after the accident he couldn't walk at all. He wasn't even able to sit up on his own when a visitor came. And he couldn't even feel his legs when doctors touched them. But when he put on the robotic suit, he was able to stand up and walk on his own again. He isn't able to walk at all without the suit. Robotics changed his life.

Host: So, people have a much better quality of life thanks to these new types of robots?

Professor: Yeah, that's right. Service robots are also very helpful to people.

Host: What do service robots do?

Professor: Well, one of the reasons that service robots were invented is to save people time. They do all the jobs around the house that people find difficult, dirty, or boring. For instance, robots can put clothes into a washing machine, plates and cups into a dishwasher, and they can clean your kitchen and bathroom. But for some people, service robots are really important; they're not just a **luxury**. Elderly people, for example, can't always do housework easily. They might need help from robots. The robot means they are able to stay in their own homes for longer.

Host: So, robots can help people in their everyday life, but how do they help more generally?

Professor: Robots are now solving modern problems, too. Have you heard of robotic fish?

Host: I haven't, but I guess they are robots that swim in water. What do they do?

Professor: They were developed to help scientists with information collection. They look like fish, they swim and move like other fish, but when they are swimming, they can **collect information** about the amount of pollution in the water. Scientists can find out about pollution quickly due to the robotic fish.

Host: Well, I have heard of robots that clean your house, so it's good to know they can help keep the environment clean, too. OK, we have some questions coming in, so let's hear the first one …

🔊 3.5

1 You will hear main ideas and additional information.
2 You will hear main ideas as well as additional information.

🔊 3.6

News reporter: For a long time, people have asked the same question: Do computers stop us from learning and developing? Do they make us **stupid**? A recent study at Columbia University in New York City looked at this question, in particular how computers affect our **memory**. They wanted to find out if computers have changed the way we remember information.

First, the scientists did **research** on what happens when people are asked **difficult** questions. They found that what we think when we hear difficult questions has changed because of websites like Google™. When people were asked difficult questions in the past, scientists believe they tried to think of the answer to the question. However, because of modern technology, the first thing people think about now is how to find the answer; they don't try to answer it themselves. For example, they think about what they might put into Google™, but in the past they thought about the question itself. Second, scientists found that computers have changed the type of information we remember. There are advantages and disadvantages to these changes. A disadvantage is that it seems that people now forget facts, especially if they know the information will be saved in a **file**. On the other hand, an advantage is that they

remember the **location** of the fact; in other words, where to find it. In one test, scientists told university students some facts and also where the facts were saved in a file. Most of the students couldn't remember the facts, but they were able to remember the files and the location of the facts.

In conclusion, it seems that computers are not making us stupid, but they are making us lazy! Scientists believe that we are spending time remembering where and how we can find things, but we're not trying to remember the information itself anymore.

🔊 3.7

1 When people were asked difficult questions in the past, scientists believe they tried to think of the answer to the question. However, because of modern technology, the first thing people think about now is how to find the answer …
2 For example, they think about what they might put into Google™, but in the past they thought about the question itself.
3 … it seems that people now forget facts, especially if they know the information will be saved in a file. On the other hand, an advantage is they remember the location of the fact; in other words, where to find it.
4 In conclusion, it seems that computers are not making us stupid, but they are making us lazy!

🔊 3.8

Mandy: I take notes on my laptop in class. If the professor writes a lot of information on the whiteboard, I take a photo of it and paste it into my notes. The laptop is useful for the Internet, too. In my history class, the instructor often refers to websites. In my notes, I insert links so that I can find them again later.

Feng: I use my laptop mainly in my English class. We write papers in class, and then we upload them to a class folder. We also share documents and presentations. If the professor assigns a group presentation, we can all work on it from home. Sometimes two or three people are editing a document at the same time.

Erica: My French teacher recommended a website for learning vocabulary. You type in the words you want to learn ... and the definitions, and it makes flashcards ... and quizzes. You can download them and print them out. It's an app, too, so you can put the flashcards on your phone. So you can learn vocabulary anywhere. It's really useful.

Armando: It's difficult for me to focus when I'm using my computer to study. I keep checking social media. But I found an app that blocks all that stuff ... text messages, social media sites, whatever you want. You choose the sites that you want to block and for how long. Now I use it all the time, and I don't get distracted.

UNIT 4

▶ The Impact of Oceans on Climate

Water covers almost 70% of the Earth. But it doesn't just stay in the same place.

Like the air above it, the water in the oceans moves around the planet. It moves because the Earth is spinning, and this has a big effect on our climate.

The spinning of the Earth causes large circles of currents in the oceans. These circular currents are called "ocean gyres." North of the equator, they move clockwise. South of the equator, they move in the opposite direction. These gyres move water and heat. That's why they are important to our climate.

Ocean currents move lots of energy and heat away from the equator. This changes our climate. For example, warmer water from the equator moves thousands of miles north. The result is warmer weather there.

South of the equator, ocean gyres are also important. They move cooler water north along the west coast of Chile in South America.

This water has lots of food in it, so it's a perfect place for fish to live. In fact, 20% of the fish we catch for food comes from this small part of the ocean.

Without these ocean gyres, our world would be a very different place.

🔊 **4.1**

1 **A:** Did you know global warming is still increasing?

  B: Is it?

2 **A:** It's my birthday today.

  B: Really? Happy birthday!

3 **A:** The weather got really chilly, didn't it?

  B: I suppose so.

4 **A:** Thanks for inviting me to your party!

  B: You're welcome. It'll be nice to see you!

5 **A:** Dinner was great.

  B: Good. Glad you liked it.

🔊 **4.2**

Sergio: So we need to think of some questions for this survey about the weather, Murat. Should we brainstorm a list of them?

Murat: I think we should decide what we want to find out. Professor Hadland told us we should look at all the different things we could survey, group them, and then try to choose the most important ones.

Sergio: Right. Effects of weather on mood.

Murat: Well, we're looking at weather in North America, especially the northwestern coast where it is often cold and wet. Generally in North America people see sunshine as positive, which I find strange. In my country, it's hot all the time, so we like **cool** days. But anyway ... I read some research about weather and moods in Canada. But it had so many different answers it wasn't clear that weather changes people's mood.

Sergio: Oh … great …

Murat: But they did find *some* specific results: They noticed that good, **dry**, sunny weather didn't make people happier. But bad weather made people more **upset** if they were already unhappy.

Sergio: And … ?

Murat: And, therefore, unhappy people felt even worse when it was wet and windy.

Sergio: Oh, OK. So for the "good weather" category – no link. But for the "bad weather" part – it causes unhappy people to feel worse.

Murat: Yes. And the amount of sunlight seems to be linked to feeling tired. When it is sunny, people have more **energy** and are less tired.

Sergio: OK, I've added that.

Murat: Also, I read something about **humid** weather. Another experiment showed that really humid weather changes how we work. As a result, it is more difficult to work and it's hard to pay attention. And there was something about heat and anger. Really hot weather can make people angrier, I think.

Sergio: Are you sure? Should I add it?

Murat: Well, write it down anyway.

Sergio: OK, which area do you think we should look at then?

Murat: I think the humid one is important. Especially for students.

Sergio: But the one on bad weather making people feel worse could be interesting, too; it sounds like there are more useful facts with that topic.

Murat: Yeah, true. I'm not sure about the really hot weather and being **angry**; I can't remember if that's true. So let's leave that out. That leaves three possible topics – humid weather stops us working, or sunny weather makes us less tired, or bad weather makes people feel worse.

Sergio: Hmm, the one about humid weather looks at how people study. It isn't really about how people feel, so it isn't useful for us. I'd go with bad weather or sunny weather.

Murat: I see what you mean. We could choose either of those. I'm not sure about the bad weather one. It's kind of depressing, isn't it? Which do you **prefer**?

Sergio: I don't really care.

Murat: Well, if you don't care, let's do the one about sunshine and having energy. It's more positive.

🔊 **4.3**

Murat: … and so I put all the results into a spreadsheet on my laptop. Here are all the answers from the surveys I did, 12 of them. Oh, and the three surveys that you did.

Sergio: Yeah. OK … let's see what they say.

Murat: We asked about how people felt when they woke up on a sunny day.

Sergio: And?

Murat: Fourteen out of fifteen people said they feel better in sunny weather than when it is very wet or rainy. They prefer sunshine.

Sergio: OK.

Murat: And 13 of them said it made them feel they could get a lot done that day. Also 12 out of 15 people said that they did more when the weather was good.

Sergio: What about when they feel most tired?

Murat: Well, everyone said that they felt tired if the weather was cloudy and dark. And 14 said they had the most energy when there was lots of light.

Sergio: So, good weather means that people have more energy.

Murat: Yeah, that is what our survey seems to show. Of course, it might be different in another country. Maybe it depends on the place you live …

🔊 **4.4**

Reporter: Global warming is an important issue around the world. Recently it has created problems in the Western Ghats rainforests of India. Forests are important for slowing down global warming because of the work that trees do for us. Trees are global cleaners: They take in carbon dioxide (CO_2), the gas that heats the atmosphere. So every time we cut down trees, we make global warming worse. Then global warming damages the forests more. More trees **disappear** because the changes in temperature stop the normal growth of the forest. Nowadays rainforests get less rain, and this is changing the way they work.

Governments around the world are beginning to work on the problem. Although governments say they will stop the damage to forests, scientists don't think the work is happening quickly enough. The scientists say the forests are changing. The animals, and the plants that animals need, are changing. In fact, scientists **believe** 45% of the forest areas are going to change completely in the next 80 years.

This is where the purple frog **becomes** important. A report tells us that the frog is in danger of disappearing forever. The frog can run very fast, makes a noise like a small chicken, and is one of the most **unusual** animals in the world. Of course, for some people, the end of one type of frog is not important. But it is for Biju Das, a researcher from Delhi University who **discovered** it in 2003. For him, the problems of the purple frog show what global warming is doing to the Indian rainforests. He explains that this interesting animal won't be around much longer if we don't **take care of** the forests.

Mr. Das is going to present information about the forests next week. During the next week, many people are meeting to talk about the climate and **saving** the rainforests. According to Mr. Das, we need to plan now, or we will probably lose some species completely. If we don't think **carefully** about the climate of the forests, the purple frog possibly won't be around for much longer. On to the weather report now …

🔊 **4.5**

1 It is more difficult to work in high humidity, so our concentration drops.

2 People feel more energy in sunny weather. Therefore, they can get a lot done if the sun is shining.

3 Some countries are really hot and don't get much rain. As a result, there isn't enough water for people to drink.

🔊 **4.6**

Interviewer: For most students, time management is a big challenge. And here to give us some advice about time management are Grace and Roberto, both senior-year students. Welcome.

Grace: Thanks!

Roberto: Thank you.

Interviewer: So, Grace … let's start with you. What was the biggest difficulty that you had in managing your time?

Grace: Well, when I started college, I couldn't believe how much free time I had. Compared with high school … you know … where every minute of the day is organized for you? In college I only had to go to a couple of classes a day! It was awesome! But then about halfway through the semester, I realized I was supposed to be studying the rest of the time! So I had to work like crazy to catch up.

Interviewer: I can imagine! What about you, Roberto? Did you have the same kind of problem?

Roberto: Yeah, I actually joined a lot of clubs and organizations. I was always busy … I didn't have time to study! At first it was fun, but then it became really stressful.

Interviewer: So ... what advice would you give to new college students?

Roberto: Don't try to do everything! Be realistic about what you can do.

Grace: Yes. Professors expect you to work a lot outside of class.

Roberto: Use a planner. You have to plan when you're going to study ... especially for exams.

Interviewer: That's good advice.

Grace: I agree. I use my planner all the time. It's also important to know what the best time for you to study is. Like, after two years I finally realized that I don't do my best work late in the evening! The best time for me to study is probably the morning. So now I try to schedule my classes for the afternoon and the evening, and study in the mornings.

Roberto: Yeah. Work out the time that is best for you ... . Oh, and one more thing. Take breaks! Don't think you can study effectively for six hours straight!

UNIT 5

▶ **Kasparov versus Deep Blue**

Narrator: Humans began playing chess in northern India nearly 1,500 years ago. But we only recently began competing against computers.

Garry Kasparov is one of the greatest world chess champions in history. In the 1990s, he played a famous match against an IBM super computer. The computer's name was Deep Blue.

To play chess well, you need many different skills.

But computers can only calculate numbers. Kasparov started the first game. An engineer from IBM moved the chess pieces for Deep Blue.

A chess genius like Kasparov can think about three moves a second.

But in that same second, the computer is able to process 200 million possible moves. Garry Kasparov played the first game very well.

It took nearly four hours. In the end, the computer lost.

Commentator: And Garry Kasparov has won the first game against Deep Blue in fantastic style.

Narrator: But the second game was different. Kasparov tried to trick Deep Blue into a mistake. But the computer didn't make a move.

It was quiet for 15 minutes. It seemed like the computer was thinking.

It wasn't tricked. Instead, it made a great move of its own.

This time the human was losing to the machine.

Kasparov tried to escape, but he couldn't. For the first time in history, a computer beat the world chess champion.

Commentator: And Kasparov has resigned.

🔊 5.1

1 The teacher's name isn't Mr. Rosso. It's Mr. Rosson.

2 I took a golf lesson, not a tennis lesson.

3 The game is at 6:00 tonight, not 6:30, so don't be late.

4 Yasmin doesn't take drama classes, she takes gymnastics classes.

5 The competition will be in Colombia, not in Brazil.

🔊 5.2

Yasmin: For my project I looked at some unusual sports that people play around the world. These aren't team sports. Instead people compete to win individually. I'd like to start by talking about chess boxing. You may already know about the two sports. Chess is a game played with a board and different chess pieces. Very intelligent people often play this game because players need to think very carefully. Boxing is a totally different kind of sport, though; being **strong** is more important because boxers have to hit each other. They wear gloves and helmets in the ring, but it's still difficult. Now "chess boxing" is a new type of sport where the players do both activities. They start with boxing, sorry, I mean chess, and then do some boxing and they continue doing each activity back and forth – alternating. The person who wins the boxing match or the chess game first is the **champion**. One benefit of this sport is that it gives people a chance to **compete** physically and mentally. It isn't just thinking or physical activity; it's both.

Another sport that challenges people is urban golf. Urban golf is similar to normal golf, but you don't need to go to a golf course. You get clubs and a golf ball – well, actually, it is a soft tennis ball instead of a hard golf ball. Then you can play in the street, which is why it is called "urban," If you play urban golf, you don't need to go anywhere special or need much money to play. You just agree where you want to **hit** the ball, for example, a sign in the street or a trash can. On the other hand, **intelligent** players know that you may break something if you hit the ball too hard, so they try to play fairly carefully.

Next, I'd like to talk about the Moroccan desert footrace, which is also called the *Marathon des Sables*, or the Sahara Marathon. This race is held every year over a week, or rather over six days. The runners have to be really strong. On the longest day, the runners have to run 57 miles – that's 92 kilometers. The best thing about it is that the champion can say he or she has won the hardest marathon in the world.

Finally, I'd like to look at Sepak Takraw. This is a type of volleyball and is very popular in Southeast Asia. The players use a different kind of ball, and they can use their feet to **kick** the ball or hit it with their knees, chest, or head. The sport began in Indonesia and it – no, not Indonesia – it began in Malaysia, although it is also very popular in Thailand and Indonesia. One good thing about Sepak Takraw is that it is now played in schools in many countries, including Canada, and gets children to play sports.

🔊 **5.3**

1 Now "chess boxing" is a new type of sport where the players do both activities. They start with boxing, sorry, I mean chess, and then do some boxing, and they continue doing each activity back and forth – alternating.

2 Urban golf is similar to normal golf, but you don't need to go to a golf course. You get clubs and a golf ball – well, actually, it is a soft tennis ball instead of a hard golf ball.

3 Next, I'd like to talk about the Moroccan desert footrace, which is also called the *Marathon des Sables*, or the Sahara Marathon. This race is held every year over a week, or rather over six days.

4 Finally, I'd like to look at Sepak Takraw. This is a type of volleyball and is very popular in Southeast Asia. The players use a different kind of ball, and they can use their feet to kick the ball or hit it with their knees, chest, or head. The sport began in Indonesia and it – no, not Indonesia – it began in Malaysia, although it is also very popular in Thailand and Indonesia.

🔊 **5.4**

Chen: Andre, I know you played on a college soccer team, so I'd like to ask your opinion about something. Do you think the Olympic athletes and other athletes like soccer and tennis players are too focused on getting money from companies? Every time I turn on the TV, I see a famous athlete in a commercial for some product. Those athletes are getting paid a huge amount of money to be in advertisements. It seems like the athletes are more interested in making money than in representing their countries. I think there is definitely more marketing and business in sports than ever before. As a longtime sports **fan**, I really think all this money and advertising from big companies is taking something away from sports and **competitions**.

Andre: Well, I would say that all athletes, even the rich and famous ones, are still really focused on the sport. Without the sport, they have no job! And athletes who aren't famous, or are only somewhat famous, deserve to make all the money they can. Many athletes devote their whole lives to training. How can they live, work, and pay for training all by themselves? Being an athlete, especially one who doesn't get paid, is really expensive. The **cost** of training is really high, and athletes need to spend a lot of time training to be good at a sport.

So big companies might give money to sports teams and individual athletes to help them train. In some competitions, like the Olympics, there are both professional players and amateurs – you know, people who do the sport as a hobby and not as a job. I think both should be able to get **support** from companies. Look at Novak Djokovic. He's a Serbian tennis player who is paid money by a clothing company to wear their clothes and be in their ads. Other companies support him, too. Without all the help from companies, he might not have enough money to play tennis as his "job." Having that time and money allows him to be such a good tennis player!

Chen: But when a big company pays a team or an athlete, it makes them wear the company name and designs, and they sign contracts … isn't that really like being an employee and working for a company? To me, these athletes work in advertising and marketing!

Andre: You have a point, but if the athletes don't get good training, they might not **score** a lot of points and do well in competitions. If that happens, they can lose their chance to make a lot of money after the competitions are over. And actually, only about 5 percent of Olympic athletes get money from big companies to be in ads.

Chen: That doesn't sound fair. Shouldn't countries pay their own athletes a **salary** to train? After all, they *do* represent the countries. I read that in the U.K., the government pays the country's Olympic athletes to train, so there is less pressure there to get money from a company. Also, there are **prizes** for all the competitions, and sometimes that gives them extra money.

Andre: Well, obviously poorer countries can't usually pay the costs for training athletes. And of course, the countries with lots of money can train their athletes really well. If companies are supporting lots of athletes, more people can participate in competitions.

Chen: Still, I think all this money takes something away from the Olympics and other sporting events. We see ads almost everywhere!

Andre: But being in a commercial is a great opportunity for the athlete and the business. If an athlete lets his or her face be on a cereal box or wears some clothing with a company's name on it, people will probably buy the product. So it is good for the company, and the athlete gets more money to train with. I also think that all the ads at big competitions like the Olympics or the World Cup help lower the ticket prices for fans, so the competitions don't have to **charge** so much. It's good for everyone!

Chen: Hmm … I'm not sure if I agree with you, but I understand your point.

🔊 **5.5**

1 I think there is definitely more marketing and business in sports than ever before.

2 And actually, only about 5 percent of Olympic athletes get money from companies to be in ads.

3 Well, obviously poorer countries can't usually pay the costs for training athletes.

4 And of course, the countries with lots of money can train their athletes really well.

🔊 **5.6**

Professor: OK everyone, as you know, you have a midterm exam in class next Friday. So please make sure that you come to class on time.

Student 1: Can we use our laptops, or is it on paper?

Professor: It's a pen-and-paper test. So you don't need your laptops.

Student 2: Is it OK to use dictionaries?

Professor: Yes, you may use dictionaries.

Student 3: How long will it take?

Professor: About an hour. That will be plenty of time.

Student 2: What kind of test is it?

Professor: Well, there are five questions that you will need to answer. You will write a paragraph for each question.

Student 1: How should we prepare?

Professor: Well, you should read chapters 5 and 6 in the textbook and study the definitions at the end of each chapter. They will definitely be on the test.

Student 2: What percentage of our grade is it?

Professor: This test counts for 40 percent of your final grade.

UNIT 6

▶ **Food at Coffee Shops**

Narrator: Starbucks and Costa Coffee are two of the biggest coffee shop chains in the world. But in England, Caffè Nero is growing quickly and has now opened up its first American stores in Boston, Massachusetts.

Gerry Ford: We didn't look at Costa or Starbucks and try to mimic them at all or do anything similar. And, for better or for worse, we kind of marched to our own drum.

Narrator: Gerry Ford started Caffè Nero in London, but his stores use an Italian model. Coffee is the most important item, but coffee shops only really do well if they can get their customers to spend money on food, like sandwiches and cookies.

Gerry Ford: The driving force is the core product of coffee and the craftsmanship and the quality that goes into that, but the food sort of complements that. We have 30% of our sales, um, are in food, which is higher than either of the other two major brands, and higher than most local independents.

Narrator: Lunchtime at Caffè Nero stores is always busy.

At the London headquarters, food consultant Ursula Ferrigno helps Caffè Nero give their food some real Italian flavor. But what kind of food do customers want the most?

In the end, this British company has found a successful business model selling Americanized Italian food and good quality coffee.

🔊 **6.1**

1 forty-eight percent

2 a half / one half

3 a fifth / one fifth

4 thirty-one point five

5 a hundred three / one hundred and three / one oh three

6 one thousand, five hundred forty / one thousand, five hundred and forty

7 six thousand one / six thousand and one

🔊 6.2

Prof. Gould: OK, Alika. Should we look at your **project** now?

Alika: OK, yeah.

Prof. Gould: You've done a lot of reading for this, which is great. I can see you wrote a lot of information down.

Alika: Yeah, I haven't finished yet – I ran out of time. But I read as much as I could – about 103 different reports. I took part in the discussions on this with students from my study group. I studied the way people work.

Prof. Gould: Good. Can you tell me what you learned?

Alika: Well, I looked at how people **spend time** at work. I was interested in how people **wasted time** and why they didn't work hard at their jobs; I mean, the reasons why they didn't focus on their work. I found out a lot of interesting information. For example, almost half of the workers wasted time on the Internet. They were surfing the Internet or writing personal emails. It was 48 percent of workers, in fact. 31.5 percent also said they spent time talking to **colleagues** instead of working. And a little under half that amount, 15 percent, said they took longer coffee and lunch **breaks** than they should. Only 5 percent said they spent time texting friends and making plans for after work.

Prof. Gould: Good. And did you find out the reasons why?

Alika: Yeah. Approximately half said they didn't work hard because they weren't happy with their jobs.

Prof. Gould: I see.

Alika: And about a third, 33.5 percent, thought they didn't **earn** a good enough salary. They said they didn't have enough money for vacations or nice clothes. They had just enough money to get by, so they didn't work as hard as they could. Some

people, about 19 percent, said they had to work too many hours.

Prof. Gould: So, what are some effects of people not working very hard?

Alika: Hmm ... if people aren't working hard, companies don't get what they are paying for.

Prof. Gould: Can you give me some examples?

Alika: Well, when people don't work hard, productivity goes down. Because productivity is how fast workers make things or do services, if workers are not working hard, the company doesn't make a **profit**. Then they can't pay higher salaries.

🔊 6.3

Joe: Hi, Sam. Good to see you again.

Sam: Hello, Joe.

Joe: So, last time we met we talked about your business **goals**. Was it useful?

Sam: Useful? ... Yeah, it was. You really made me think! But now I have a lot of **stress** about losing money.

Joe: Oh, yeah? Why are you stressed about that?

Sam: Well, I realized how many **weaknesses** a business can have! One **careless** mistake, and I could lose a lot of money.

Joe: Exactly! But there are things you think will cause you to lose money?

Sam: Well, when we looked at the company's **strengths** and weaknesses, we talked about the quality and happiness of my workers, the costs of running the business, and reaching new **customers** to help grow the business. Each of these areas could be a way to help make money or a way to lose money if you don't have a good plan.

Joe: Wow – very good! Those are all important to think about. Is there anything else?

Sam: And what else was there? Oh, of course, customers!

Joe: Well, that gives us plenty to talk about today! So, let's think about what you can do for your employees. You said that your workers were unhappy and not working hard enough. Keeping your employees happy will make them more likely to work hard for the business. Try organizing some social events once a month during work hours. That could be a good first step! Also, maybe you should paint the walls a brighter color. The office is really dark, and people feel like they're in a cave. Brighter colors can help make people happier. And happier employees will also work harder.

Sam: Oh, OK. Well, that's good to know.

Joe: You also have to cut costs. You spend way too much money on electricity every month. Turn off the lights and computers at the end of the workday. You should also find some cheaper parts for your products that are still well made. It's a tough job, but I can help you find them.

Sam: I see. That would be great!

Joe: If you spend less money, you can make a better profit. You have some excellent ads. But you mentioned that you are having trouble reaching new customers, and growing your number of customers is really important for a successful business. So if I were you, I would try adding online sales to get more customers.

Sam: Yeah, I like that idea. I have a website already, but it looks pretty old and **messy**.

Joe: But there are things we can work on. If you want to sell online, you should start by making sure that the website doesn't look messy. If you don't have the **skills** to make it look neat, hire a professional web designer! You want a neat, clean website. It isn't something you want to be careless with.

Sam: I see. Well, I would like to have a lot of black on the website. I think that color is professional and serious looking.

Joe: I understand. But I think if you are marketing to women mostly, you need to use more blue. Lots of women say that blue is their favorite color. Men like it, too, so it's a good color.

Sam: Uh-huh … That's a good idea. I actually like blue, too. I think someone else told me about colors people prefer, but I forgot.

Joe: Yeah. It's easy to forget to think about something as simple as color. So for our next meeting, you should create your website design and bring a plan. You could think about how it looks, as well as what it says. You don't want it to look … well, you would want to be sure it looks well organized and the best it can be. It should also be really easy to use. Next time we'll go over your design and see how to make it better. We will also think about hiring a good web designer to make your website look great and be easy to use.

Sam: OK, great! I'll do that and bring it in next week.

🔊 6.4

Joe: Hi, Sam. Good to see you again.

Sam: Hello, Joe.

Joe: So, last time we met we talked about your business goals. Was it useful?

Sam: Useful? … Yeah, it was. You really made me think! But now I have a lot of stress about losing money.

Joe: Oh, yeah? Why are you stressed about that?

Sam: Well, I realized how many weaknesses a business can have! One careless mistake, and I could lose a lot of money.

Joe: Exactly! But there are things you think will cause you to lose money?

Sam: Well, when we looked at the company's strengths and weaknesses, we talked about the quality and happiness of my workers, the costs of running the business, and reaching new customers to help grow the business. Each of these areas could be a way to help make money or a way to lose money if you don't have a good plan.

Joe: Wow – very good! Those are all important to think about. Is there anything else?

🔊 6.5

Joe: Exactly! But there are things you think will cause you to lose money?

🔊 6.6

a Was it useful?

b Exactly! But there are things you think will cause you to lose money?

c Oh, yeah?

d Well, when we look at the company's strengths and weaknesses ...

e Why are you stressed about that?

f Useful? ... Yeah, it was.

🔊 6.7

Alex: I really like classes where we do a lot of projects and group work. It's much more interesting when you actually do something ... when you don't just read the textbook. You participate more. And also ... I think it's important to learn how to work with other people because when you are working in a job, that's the way it is. You have to work in teams all the time. If you don't get along, you have to work it out. Actually I've made some really good friends from working on class projects! It's a good way to get to know other people in your class.

Yuki: I really don't like group work ... I've never had a good experience with it. I feel like we waste so much time deciding what to do and who's going to do it. And then when we *do* meet, people come late, and want to chat, and they don't focus on the work, so we have to have *more* meetings ... Arrgh! Plus, some people never do anything. Or ... you depend on them to do something and then they don't do it. It always seems like the same two people do all of the work for the whole group. I prefer to work by myself because I really don't have time to do a lot of extra work outside of class.

UNIT 7

▶ **Trash Artists**

Narrator: Kiwayu Island is located off the coast of Kenya in the Indian Ocean.

There aren't many tourists on these beautiful beaches.

The people who live here seem very isolated from the rest of the world. But they are actually connected to the rest of the world in a surprising way.

Plastic and other trash from around the Indian Ocean washes up onto the beach daily. So every day the women of Kiwayu go to the beach to pick up trash. Why? To earn a living. They collect flip-flops and bring them to their villages. There, artists and craftsmen turn the trash into colorful ornaments and souvenirs to sell.

The people of Kiwayu make good money this way. They send most of their ornaments to Nairobi, the capital of Kenya. These are then exported to stores around the world or sold on the Internet.

Woman: Some people here didn't have houses before, but now they do. Some people didn't have animals for food, but now they do.

Now we can buy a lot of things. Some of us couldn't send our children to school, but now we can. That's the most important thing for me.

🔊 **7.1**

Student Presenter: Hello, everyone. So in this presentation I'd like to discuss the designers of some everyday objects: Arne Jacobsen, James Dyson, and Sir Jonathan Ive. These people designed **simple** things that have changed our lives and how we do everyday things. Today we are going to think about these inventors and designers, their **achievements**, and how their **inventions** and **designs** have helped us.

I would like to start with Arne Jacobsen, who was born in Denmark in 1902. When he was a child, he loved to paint, but his father thought being an artist wasn't a good career. So Jacobsen became a designer of many things, including buildings and furniture. For example, here is a chair he designed in 1958. It's called the "egg chair." Have any of you seen this kind of a chair before?

Razia: I have. Did they call it the "egg chair" because of its shape? It's an interesting design.

Student Presenter: Yes, you have a good **point**. I think it was called that because of the egg-like shape. Nowadays, we still see Jacobsen's designs around us. When you look at the chair design, can you guess what Jacobsen was like as a person?

Razia: His chair looks like a simple, neat design. So maybe he liked simple and neat things, and not **complicated** things.

Student Presenter: Actually, that's right. He did. For example, when he was growing up, he painted his room white because he didn't like all the flowers on the wallpaper he had. And as an adult, he worked hard to make his designs perfect. In fact, he often kept his workers at work until late, trying to make things better. But even though he worked hard, Jacobsen liked to joke and do funny things. For instance, as a child he liked to play jokes on others, and as an adult he once wore a melon for a hat when someone dared him to. He also liked working on his own projects in his free time and found painting to be relaxing. These days, Jacobsen is famous for his modern, simple designs. His work showed that he thought about the **purpose** that his designs would serve for people.

Next, I'd like to talk about an inventor, James Dyson. Can anyone think of something you often use that might have his last name, Dyson, on it?

Razia: I know, a vacuum cleaner!

Ebru: Or a hand dryer?

Student Presenter: Both of those things are correct. Dyson's designs and inventions are made to solve problems. His ideas come because he sees things that could work better, like the vacuum cleaner and hand dryer. But how did he start? Well, Dyson was born in England in 1947. His father died when he was only nine. As a result, Dyson ended up becoming someone who never gave up. He studied art and design before he studied engineering. When he saw something that didn't work well, he got frustrated and worked to improve it. For example, his first invention was a wheelbarrow with a ball for a wheel. This made it easier to carry heavy things in the garden and over rough ground. It was an interesting new **use** for a ball. Also, even though he changed majors, he was still interested in art as well as designing. Take a look at this photo. What do you see?

Ebru: It looks like a waterfall made from glass and water, with the water running up instead of falling down. That's surprising.

Student Presenter: That's right. This was a piece of art that Dyson made in 2003, called *Wrong Garden*. It tricks the eye. This shows Dyson's love of good design as well as being an inventor. Dyson is still inventing new things. But he is also interested in supporting education for students, and gives money to schools to help students study so they might become inventors, too. He has even donated money to the University of Cambridge to support students and research there with a focus on technology.

Now, I have one last picture to show you. It's a phone with a special design. It's called the iPhone. I think a lot of us know about this phone. It was designed by Sir Jonathan Ive for Apple. He is responsible for a lot of Apple's product designs, which are simple, clean, and thin. Ive has won a lot of awards for his Apple designs, and you can see a lot of his work in museums, too. He is from London, and he was made a Knight Commander of the British Empire in 2013 for his design work. He is known as being hard working and creative. I think that his designs will continue to influence the way we live and work for a long time!

🔊 7.2

Yasmin: Hello.

Luisa: Hi, Yasmin. It's Luisa.

Yasmin: Hi, Luisa! How are you?

Luisa: OK, I guess. Actually, I'm not that great.

Yasmin: Oh, no! What's up? Is something wrong?

Luisa: It's the presentation for class. You know, the one on **remarkable** people who have done something really interesting or unusual. I'm having trouble doing it. Have you finished it yet?

Yasmin: Yeah, I have. I just have to write a conclusion.

Luisa: Good for you. I bet it's really good.

Yasmin: Thanks Luisa. I'm pretty happy with it, but the introduction's not great. It needs a little more work. How much have you done?

Luisa: Well ... I haven't done all of it ...

Yasmin: All? Or any of it?

Luisa: I'm not very good at finding things to present. I'm having trouble thinking of ideas. Who did you do yours on?

Yasmin: I chose Jonathan Koon. He's a remarkable man.

Luisa: Who's he? Why are you interested in him?

Yasmin: Well, his parents came to the U.S. from Hong Kong, and he was born in the U.S. in 1983. He grew up in New York. By the time he was 16, he was a millionaire.

Luisa: How did he do that?

Yasmin: Well, during the 90s, he was bringing special car parts from Asia to sell in the U.S., and he had a lot of **success**. But then he started college and closed his business while he was going to classes. After he graduated with a business degree in 2004, he started his business again. He was very successful and even invented some other things that could be added to cars to make them more useful, like a cell phone holder.

Luisa: That's great that he became really successful so young. Is there anything else about his life that's **amazing**?

Yasmin: Well, it was also unusual how he expanded his business because he didn't always sell car parts. In 2008 he bought a clothing brand from the famous American rap star, JayZ. And so then he designed clothing that lots of people wore. By 2010 he was working with an Italian designer making luxury clothing. He became famous for his clothing designs. When he was 31, his companies were worth at least $80 million. Nowadays, he is even making art. He made a piece out of two beautiful Chinese vases. He smashed them and then created an egg-shaped piece of art from the pieces. It's beautiful and was sold for thousands of dollars. So, he's an **entrepreneur**, an inventor, a designer, and an artist.

Luisa: That's amazing! Wow ... I need to find someone like that.

Yasmin: Why don't you do something on Joseph Conrad? Do you know about him?

Luisa: Umm ... I don't know a lot about Conrad ... Who ... ?

Yasmin: He was a Polish writer. But he didn't write in Polish; he wrote in English.

Luisa: Umm ... His life doesn't sound that extraordinary.

Yasmin: He had a hard childhood because his parents both died. But his **situation** changed when an uncle helped him. While he was living with his uncle, he studied Latin, Greek, geography, and math. Also, I think he was a sailor before he **retired** and became a writer, but you'd need to check that.

Luisa: OK ... I'll check him out.

Yasmin: Do you know what the professor wants us to present?

Luisa: Well, I'm not sure I understand everything ...

🔊 **7.3**

1 I'm pretty happy with it.
2 He's a remarkable man.
3 That's amazing!
4 I'll check him out.

🔊 **7.4**

My presentation is about Thomas Edison. He was an American inventor, and he was born in 1847. He is a remarkable person because he invented a lot of the things we know and use every day, such as the electric light bulb. Well, he wasn't the first to invent one, but he *was* the first person to invent one that could last a long time. This was in 1879 while he was working in his research lab in Menlo Park, New Jersey. It lasted 14.5 hours! Another important example of Edison's amazing inventions is the motion picture camera. We all know this today as the video camera. Edison and his team invented it in 1891, and they showed short, six-minute movies. Equally important was Edison's work with Henry Ford, who started the Ford Motor Company. Edison was worried about America's dependence on foreign rubber for tires. So while he was working at a lab in Florida in 1927, he found a new source of rubber in local plants ...

🔊 **7.5**

Professor: All right. Next week you're going to be doing some presentations in class, and I know that this is difficult for many students ... especially if English is not your first language. So I'm going to give you three things you should do to prepare for a good presentation and then explain how you should do them. If you follow this advice, you will do well, not just in this class, but every time you have to speak in front of a group. OK, so what should you do? The first thing you need to do is practice. You should practice your speech several times before you give a presentation in class. And how should you do this? Well, practice aloud; don't just read through your notes in silence. Practice the pronunciation of key words, like ... names of people and places ... numbers ... and important terms. These need to be very clear! Speak in front of a mirror, or record yourself on video.

Next, during the presentation, remember to relate to the audience. Smile at them at the beginning ... and remember to look at them! Make eye contact with different people in the room. You can sometimes ask a question or two at the beginning, and get a response.

And finally ... and I know this is difficult ... slow down. Pause after each main point and look up at the audience. This gives them time to understand what you are saying ... and it will make your presentation much clearer.

So, just remember these three points: practice your presentation, relate to your audience, and slow down. OK? Any questions?

UNIT 8

▶ **Empire of the Sun**

Narrator: Here in the Mojave Desert in California, NASA, America's space agency, communicates with the spacecraft Voyager. Project scientist Dr. Edward Stone became part of the Voyager team before it began its journey in 1977.

Voyager's goal was to fly by the planets Jupiter, Saturn, Uranus, and Neptune, and to send back information to the Earth.

Dr. Edward Stone: None of us knew how long the spacecraft could survive.

When I started on the Voyager, my two daughters were young, and by the, and of course, by the time they were in college, we were already, er, past Saturn. We were on our way to Uranus, they got married. The Voyager just kept going. We had grandchildren, and Voyager just kept going, and so now our grandchildren are aware of what's happening to Voyager, just like our children were.

Narrator: And what's really amazing is that we're still learning new things from Voyager.

Almost 40 years later, Voyager still communicates with this dish over 11 billion miles away.

Its message travels at the speed of light, but it still takes more than 17 hours to get here.

This little green triangle shows Voyager in deep space. It is a message from the spacecraft.

In 2012, Voyager 1 left our solar system and became the first man-made object ever to travel outside the empire of the sun.

🔊 8.1

1 When the sun is out, I make sure my son uses sunscreen so he doesn't get sunburned.

2 Have you read the information about the Red Planet?

3 We are having a picnic whether it is hot or not. It has been good weather recently, so we are hoping it will be nice.

4 She ate her dinner before she went out at eight o'clock.

5 There are two doctors in the family, and their daughter is also studying medicine.

6 Our guest was in the house for an hour.

🔊 8.2

1 The weather is really nice today.

2 I waited for an hour.

3 Are you going there later?

4 I read the book yesterday.

5 We ate our dinner.

6 I don't mind.

🔊 8.3

Host: In this episode of *Astronomy Today*, we are looking at space travel and the **journeys** that people hope to make **beyond** the moon. We'll think about the **planets** people haven't visited yet and whether we are likely to visit some of them in the future. Let's begin inside our own solar system, which is made up of all the planets and the sun. Venus, Jupiter, and Neptune are probably the first names that come to mind when you think of the solar system. But the planet scientists hope to visit next is Mars. Mars is known as the "Red Planet" because of its color. NASA, the U.S. government group that studies space, so far has only sent robot explorers to Mars. But they are working to send humans to Mars and want to **reach** Mars by the 2030s. Even with the danger, many people want to travel to Mars.

🔊 8.4

Host: NASA wants to send humans to an asteroid by 2025. An asteroid is like a very large rock that goes around the sun like the planets do. First, NASA wants to send robots on a journey to reach the asteroid and take a large boulder from its surface. Once the robot takes the large boulder from the asteroid, the robot will set it on a **path** around the moon. After that, NASA wants to send people to **explore** the asteroid piece in the 2020s. They plan a journey to the boulder in a **spacecraft** named Orion. Orion won't be able to land on the **surface** of Mars, but it will travel to the asteroid boulder to get information. Orion will also help test new spacecraft and give NASA information that it needs to safely send people to Mars.

Outside our solar system, there is a place even more surprising than Mars, and many people would go there if we had the spacecraft to send them. It is usually called Lucy, but its scientific name is BPM 37093. It is actually a dead star, or a white dwarf star. It is what is left over when a star uses up all its energy. It doesn't burn anymore, but it shines with heat. But the most surprising fact is that this dead star is a huge diamond. Scientists have always known about the diamond-like white dwarf stars, which are made by heat. They are all outside our own solar system, like Lucy.

Lucy is about 2,500 miles (that's 4,000 kilometers) across, less than half as wide as Earth. Even though it is small, it weighs about as much as our sun. If Lucy were mined, there would be more diamonds found on it than all the diamonds on Earth through history. Even though it is a dead star, the dwarf star is hot. It has a temperature of about 4,900 degrees Fahrenheit (that's 2,700 degrees Celsius). But scientists call Lucy a cold star because it is only half as hot as our sun. And while the trip to explore Mars is planned for the 2030s, scientists have not found a way to travel outside our own solar system yet. Perhaps one day.

🔊 8.5

Host: Hello, everyone. We'll begin today's discussion with a look at how to pay for space exploration. We'll also **evaluate** the benefits of space exploration and whether the money we spend is worth it. We will first look at the **options** for paying for space exploration. I have three **experts** with me today: Dorota Loy, an engineer from the Space Development Project; Raj Padow, a researcher in economics; and Dr. Chen Wu, who is a professor of astrophysics. Let me ask Dr. Wu to start us off by giving us a little information about the impact of space exploration and the importance of spending money on it.

🔊 8.6

Host: Let me ask Dr. Wu to start us off by giving us a little information about the impact of space exploration and the importance of spending money on it.

Chen: Thanks for having me. Well, to answer your question, space exploration is important because we do research and get information about many things. For example, as scientists explore space, we learn about biology and about physics, as well as space. So for me, the most important thing is that governments give enough money for future exploration.

Dorota: You have a point that space exploration is used for a lot of scientific study. But it is very expensive, and there is less **public** money to pay for it nowadays. Is having the government pay really the only option for paying for space exploration?

Chen: I hear what you're saying, Dorota. It isn't cheap to run space programs, but the money we spend is certainly worth it. Government and public money must be included. So far, space exploration has shown us many things about how space works, what stars do, the effects on people who stay in space for a long time, and so on. We must continue to do this work so that we can explore places in space farther away and –

Raj: Can I just say something here?

Host: Yes, Raj?

Raj: I agree 100 percent with Dr. Wu that we need space exploration. But even he says it is very expensive. I know that we have to spend money to develop our space programs, and we need more money than governments have. So for me, an alternative would be to bring in thinkers from different industries to discuss different ways to pay. If we are exploring space, we could have **private** companies pay for it. For me, this is the main reason we –

Chen: But Raj, space exploration is so important. Governments must –

Raj: Sorry, Dr. Wu, can I finish my point? If so much money is spent on space exploration, the most important thing should be finding money from places other than the government. It shouldn't be just taxpayers paying for it. Private companies make lots of money from the discoveries made in space exploration, so they should pay for the costs.

Host: Dorota, you haven't said much so far. Any thoughts?

Dorota: Well, I personally don't see a problem. Dr. Wu has a good point about public government money, and I feel exactly the same as Raj about private money. But we can do both of these things – public, or government money, helps us keep the people who know the most, like those at NASA, focused on the research, and private money helps bring in other **talent** from companies that would also like to explore space, such as Virgin Galactic or SpaceX. Companies like these have already spent a lot of money on this important type of travel –

Chen: Yeah, – important space travel that governments should ...

Dorota: Please allow me to finish. There are also other choices that neither of you have talked about yet. Space exploration benefits the world. What about money from private people? There are wealthy people around the world that might be interested in giving money for these projects. Also, with the Internet, people from around the world could give money for these projects. Lots of people could make donations directly to their favorite projects. I think in the future we can get money for space exploration from more than one place. We should study these different ways and use the best solution.

Host: Dr. Wu, Raj Padow, let's get your thoughts on this. Do you agree with these ideas for paying for space exploration?

Chen: Yes ... Dorota could be right. Space exploration needs money to come from many places, as long as the government is still a part of this important area of exploration.

Raj: And I think she might be right, too. But as I said, only if there is money from private companies, too.

Host: OK, so you have some agreement here then. Let's go back to the benefits of space exploration and think about that a little more. So does anybody want to ...

🔊 **8.7**

Sergio: My astronomy professor always gives tests where we have to answer like, six questions in 45 minutes. We have to be able to think and write fast! So, to prepare for that, I think of possible questions, and practice writing the answers with a time limit. I like that, because it trains me to think and write quickly.

Li Chao: I always make an idea map when I review material for my science classes. I write a main point or idea in a circle and connect it to other ideas. I like to try to put everything on one page, and make lines to connect everything. It's a good way to summarize all the material on one page.

Anna: We have an oral exam every semester in my Italian class. We have to answer questions about the book that we read. The best way for me to prepare for that is to practice with a classmate. We think of possible questions and ask each other. It's really helpful because I review the material ... and I practice speaking at the same time!

CREDITS

The authors and publishers acknowledge the following sources of copyright material and are grateful for the permissions granted. While every effort has been made, it has not always been possible to identify the sources of all the material used, or to trace all copyright holders. If any omissions are brought to our notice, we will be happy to include the appropriate acknowledgements on reprinting and in the next update to the digital edition, as applicable.

Photo credits

Key: T = Top, C = Center, B = Below, L = Left, R = Right, BL = Below Left, BC = Below Center, BR = Below Right.

p. 12: Cultura RM Exclusive/Peter Muller/Getty Images; pp. 14–15: A Demotes/Photononstop/Getty Images; p. 19 (photo a): Danita Delimont/Gallo Images/Getty Images; p. 19 (photo b): Heracles Kritikos/Shutterstock; p. 19 (photo c): Massimo Pizzotti/Getty Images; p. 19 (photo d): Reza/Hulton Archive/Getty Images; p. 24 (photo a): Coprid/iStock/Getty Images; p. 24 (photo b): Malcolm Fife//Getty Images; p. 24 (photo c): Steve Peterson Photography/Moment/Getty Images; p. 24 (photo d): kisgorcs/iStock/Getty Images; p. 24 (photo e): Bruce Bennett/Getty Images News/Getty Images; p. 24 (photo f): Glow Décor/Glow/Getty Images; p. 24 (photo g): Mihai Andritoiu/iStock/Getty Images; p. 24 (photo h): Daly and Newton/Stone/Getty Images; p. 25: David Nunuk/All Canada Photos/Getty Images; p. 28: Frank Pali/All Canada Photos/Getty Images; pp. 36–37: Floris Leeuwenberg/Corbis Documentary/Getty Images; p. 41 (photo a): Gary Wolstenholme/Redferns/Getty Images; p. 41 (photo b): Max Dereta/Photodisc/Getty Images; p. 41 (photo c): Thomas Lohnes/Getty Images News/Getty Images; p. 47 (photo a): Ray Bradshaw/Moment/Getty Images; p. 47 (photo b): Anadolu Agency/Getty Images; p. 47 (photo c): Al Messerschmidt/Getty Images Sport/Getty Images; p. 47 (photo d): Robert Benson/Getty Images; p. 50 (T): ZUMA Press Inc/Alamy; p. 50 (B): Ryan/Beyer/The Image Bank/Getty Images; pp. 58–59: Piero Cruciatti/Alamy; p. 63 (photo a): Adrian Dennis/AFP/Getty Images; p. 63 (photo b): Huntstock/Getty Images; p. 63 (photo c): Howard Kingsnorth/The Image Bank/Getty Images; p. 63 (photo d): Kevin Schafer/Photolibrary/Getty Images; p. 63 (photo e): Pirotehnik/iStock/Getty Images; p. 69: shapecharge/E+/Getty Images; p. 78: Astrakan Images/Cultura/Getty Images; pp. 80–81: Hercules Milas/Alamy; p. 87: Eric Audras/ONOKY/Getty Images; p. 90: Hornbil Images/Alamy; p. 93 (L): Rolando Gil/The Image Bank/Getty Images; p. 93 (C): Brazil Photos/LightRocket/Getty Images; p. 93 (R): Visual China Group/Getty Images; p. 94: Bill Raften/Photolibrary/Getty Images; pp. 102–103: Pete Saloutos/Image Source/Getty Images; p. 107 (photo a): Tom Shaw/Getty Images Sport/Getty Images; p. 107 (photo b): Pierre Verdy/AFP/Getty Images; p. 107 (photo c): Nicky Loh/Getty Images Sport/Getty Images; p. 107 (photo d): Target Presse Agentur Gmbh/Getty Images News/Getty Images; p. 109: Robert Daly/Caiaimage/Getty Images; p. 115: Clive Brunskill/Getty Images Sport/Getty Images; p. 119: Feng Li/Getty Images Sport/Getty Images; p. 123 (BL), p. 137: Hero Images/Getty Images; p. 123 (BC): Hunter: Keith/Arcaid Images/Getty Images; p. 123 (BR): Spaces Images/Blend Images/Getty Images; pp. 124–125: Bloomberg/Getty Images; pp. 146–147: U.S. Coast Guard/digital version/Science Faction/Getty Images; p. 151 (photo a): MileA/iStock/Getty Images; p. 151 (photo b): Dorling Kindersley/Getty Images; p. 151 (photo c): T3 Magazine/Future/Getty Images; p. 151 (photo d): G. Jackson/Arcaid Images/Getty Images; p. 154: George C. Beresford/Hulton Archive/Getty Images; p. 157: Time & Life Pictures/The LIFE Picture Collection/Getty Images; p. 158: Moises De Pena/Getty Images Entertainment/Getty Images; p. 164: Mondadori Portfolio/Getty Images; pp. 168–169: Babak Tafreshi/Science Photo Library; p. 175: 7activestudio/iStock/Getty Images; p. 180 (T): NASA/Getty Images News/Getty Images; p. 180 (B): Mark Williamson/Oxford Scientific/Getty Images.

Front cover photographs by (man) SharpPhoto/Shutterstock and (BG) PlusONE/Shutterstock.

Illustrations

by Oxford Designers & Illustrators: pp. 34, 52, 98, 141.

Video stills supplied by BBC Worldwide Learning.

Video supplied by BBC Worldwide Learning.

Corpus

Development of this publication has made use of the Cambridge English Corpus (CEC). The CEC is a multi-billion word computer database of contemporary spoken and written English. It includes British English, American English, and other varieties of English. It also includes the Cambridge Learner Corpus, developed in collaboration with the University of Cambridge ESOL Examinations. Cambridge University Press has built up the CEC to provide evidence about language use that helps to produce better language teaching materials

Cambridge Dictionaries

Cambridge dictionaries are the world's most widely used dictionaries for learners of English. The dictionaries are available in print and online at dictionary.cambridge.org. Copyright © Cambridge University Press, reproduced with permission.

Typeset by emc design ltd

Audio production by CityVox New York

INFORMED BY TEACHERS

Classroom teachers shaped everything about *Prism*. The topics. The exercises. The critical thinking skills. The On Campus sections. Everything. We are confident that *Prism* will help your students succeed in college because teachers just like you helped guide the creation of this series.

Prism Advisory Panel

The members of the *Prism* Advisory Panel provided inspiration, ideas, and feedback on many aspects of the series. *Prism* is stronger because of their contributions.

Gloria Munson
University of Texas, Arlington

Kim Oliver
Austin Community College

Gregory Wayne
Portland State University

Julaine Rosner
Mission College

Dinorah Sapp
University of Mississippi

Christine Hagan
George Brown College/Seneca College

Heidi Lieb
Bergen Community College

Stephanie Kasuboski
Cuyahoga Community College

Global Input

Teachers from more than 500 institutions all over the world provided valuable input through:
- Surveys
- Focus Groups
- Reviews